# Math and Literature
## Grades K–1

# Math and Literature

## Grades K–1

Marilyn Burns
Stephanie Sheffield

Math Solutions Publications
Sausalito, CA

**Math Solutions Publications**
A division of
Marilyn Burns Education Associates
150 Gate 5 Road, Suite 101
Sausalito, CA 94965
www.mathsolutions.com

Portions of the present work appeared in a slightly different version in *Math and Literature (K–3), Book One* by Marilyn Burns (© 1992 by Math Solutions Publications) and *Math and Literature (K–3), Book Two* by Stephanie Sheffield (© 1995 by Math Solutions Publications).

**Library of Congress Cataloging-in-Publication Data**
Burns, Marilyn, 1941–
    Math and literature. Grades K–1 / Marilyn Burns, Stephanie Sheffield.
        p. cm.
    Includes bibliographical references and index.
      ISBN 0-941355-66-7 (alk. paper)
    1. Mathematics—Study and teaching (Primary) 2. Children's literature in mathematics education. I. Sheffield, Stephanie. II. Title.
      QA115.B957 2004
        372.7—dc22
                                    2004011479

ISBN-10: 0-941355-66-7
ISBN-13: 978-0-941355-66-7

Editor: Toby Gordon
Production: Melissa L. Inglis
Cover and interior design: Catherine Hawkes/Cat and Mouse
Composition: TechBooks

Printed in the United States of America on acid-free paper
08  07  06              ML            3  4  5

# A Message from Marilyn Burns

We at Math Solutions Professional Development believe that teaching math well calls for increasing our understanding of the math we teach, seeking deeper insights into how children learn mathematics, and refining our lessons to best promote students' learning.

Math Solutions Publications shares classroom-tested lessons and teaching expertise from our faculty of Math Solutions Inservice instructors as well as from other respected math educators. Our publications are part of the nationwide effort we've made since 1984 that now includes

- more than five hundred face-to-face inservice programs each year for teachers and administrators in districts across the country;
- annually publishing professional development books, now totaling more than fifty titles and spanning the teaching of all math topics in kindergarten through grade 8;
- four series of videotapes for teachers, plus a videotape for parents, that show math lessons taught in actual classrooms;
- on-site visits to schools to help refine teaching strategies and assess student learning; and
- free online support, including grade-level lessons, book reviews, inservice information, and district feedback, all in our quarterly *Math Solutions Online Newsletter*.

For information about all of the products and services we have available, please visit our Web site at *www.mathsolutions.com*. You can also contact us to discuss math professional development needs by calling (800) 868-9092 or by sending an e-mail to *info@mathsolutions.com*.

We're always eager for your feedback and interested in learning about your particular needs. We look forward to hearing from you.

Math Solutions®
PUBLICATIONS

# Contents

Acknowledgments                                          *ix*

Introduction by Marilyn Burns                            *xi*

*Benny's Pennies*                                         1

*The Button Box*                                          10

*Cats Add Up!*                                            15

*Inch by Inch*                                            21

*Let's Go Visiting*                                       28

*The Napping House*                                       35

*One Monday Morning*                                      45

*Pattern Fish*                                            50

*A Pig Is Big*                                            54

*Quack and Count*                                         60

*Ready or Not, Here I Come!*                              68

*Rooster's Off to See the World*                          76

*The Shape of Things*                                     81

*Six-Dinner Sid*                                          87

*Ten Black Dots*                                          92

*Ten Flashing Fireflies*                                  98

*Ten Sly Piranhas*                                        105

*A Three Hat Day*                                         108

*12 Ways to Get to 11* and *Band-Aids*                    112

*Two of Everything*                                       119

*When a Line Bends . . . a Shape Begins*                  123

*Who Sank the Boat?*                                      127

Blackline Master                                          *131*

   *Ten Flashing Fireflies* Work Mat                      *133*

References                                                *135*

Index                                                     *137*

# Acknowledgments

Special thanks to Leyani von Rotz, District Math Coordinator and Elementary Math Coach for Emery Public Schools, Emeryville, California, for creating lessons, trying them out in various classrooms, and then revising and teaching them again until they felt right. We greatly appreciate her insights, her commitment to children's learning, and her excitement about how children's books can help students learn mathematics.

Thanks to those teachers who contributed their expertise by sharing their classroom lessons with us: Marge Genolio, Jefferson Elementary School, San Francisco, California; Min Hong, P.S.11, New York, New York; Bonnie Tank, Wildwood Elementary School, Piedmont, California, and Jefferson Elementary School, San Francisco, California; Olga Torres, Mission View Elementary School, Tucson, Arizona.

Thanks to those teachers who allowed our lessons to be taught in their classrooms: Deborah Burnaman, Coleytown Elementary School, Westport, Connecticut; Joanne Downey, Mission View Elementary School, Tucson, Arizona; Mary Karnick, Beneke Elementary School, Houston, Texas; Sarah Mallow, Beneke Elementary School, Houston, Texas; Carissa Morales, Anna Yates Elementary School, Emeryville, California; Evan Pippen, Anna Yates Elementary School, Emeryville, California; and Malcolm Waugh, Anna Yates Elementary School, Emeryville, California.

# Introduction

For months before publishing this resource of classroom-tested lessons, I was surrounded by children's books. They were stacked practically up to my ears on my desk and additional piles were all around on the floor. It took some fancy shuffling at times to make space for other things that needed my attention. But I never complained. I love children's books and it was pure pleasure to be immersed in reading them and then teaching, writing, revising, and editing lessons that use them as springboards for teaching children mathematics.

This book is one in our new Math Solutions Publications series for teaching mathematics using children's literature, and I'm pleased to present the complete series:

*Math and Literature, Grades K–1*
*Math and Literature, Grades 2–3*
*Math and Literature, Grades 4–6, Second Edition*
*Math and Literature, Grades 6–8*
*Math and Nonfiction, Grades K–2*
*Math and Nonfiction, Grades 3–5*

More than ten years ago we published my book *Math and Literature (K–3)*. My premise for that book was that children's books can be effective vehicles for motivating children to think and reason mathematically. I searched for books that I knew would stimulate children's imaginations and that also could be used to teach important math concepts and skills.

After that first book's publication, my colleague Stephanie Sheffield began sending me the titles of children's books she had discovered and descriptions of the lessons she had taught based on them. Three years after publishing my book, we published Stephanie's *Math and Literature (K–3), Book Two*. And the following year we published Rusty Bresser's *Math and Literature (Grades 4–6)*, a companion to the existing books.

Over the years, some of the children's books we initially included in our resources have, sadly, gone out of print. However, other wonderful titles have emerged. For this new series, we did a thorough review of our three original resources. Stephanie and I collaborated on substantially revising our two K–3 books and reorganizing them into two different books, one for grades K–1 and the other for grades 2–3. Rusty produced a second edition of his book for grades 4–6.

In response to the feedback we received from teachers, we became interested in creating a book that would offer lessons based on children's books for middle school students, and we were fortunate enough to find two wonderful teachers, Jennifer M. Bay-Williams and Sherri L. Martinie, to collaborate on this project. I'm pleased to present their book, *Math and Literature, Grades 6–8*.

The two books that round out our series use children's nonfiction as springboards for lessons. Jamee Petersen created *Math and Nonfiction, Grades K–2*, and Stephanie Sheffield built on her experience with the Math and Literature books to team with her colleague Kathleen Gallagher to write *Math and Nonfiction, Grades 3–5*. Hearing nonfiction books read aloud to them requires children to listen in a different way than usual. With nonfiction, students listen to the facts presented and assimilate that information into what they already know about that particular subject. And rather than reading from cover to cover as with fiction, it sometimes makes more sense to read only a small portion of a nonfiction book and investigate the subject matter presented in that portion. The authors of these Math and Nonfiction books are sensitive to the demands of nonfiction and how to present new information in order to make it accessible to children.

We're still fond of the lessons that were based on children's books that are now out of print, and we know that through libraries, the Internet, and used bookstores, teachers have access to some of those books. Therefore, we've made all of the older lessons that are not included in the new series of books available online at *www.mathsolutions.com*. Please visit our Web site for those lessons and for additional support for teaching math.

I'm pleased and proud to present these new books. It was a joy to work on them, and I'm convinced that you and your students will benefit from the lessons we offer.

MARILYN BURNS
2004

Quack and Count
Seven Blind Mice
10 min till Bedtime
10 Black Dots
Splash
Sea Shapes
One to One Hundred
Ten Red Apples
Fat Frog on a Skinny Log
Mouse Counts
Feast for 10
The Shape of Things
The Icky Bug Counting Book
Just A Little Bit
One Monday Morning
Two Eyes, A Nose & a mouth
Trick or Treat
Cats Add Up!
One More Bunny
Jelly Beans for Sale (5)
When a line Bends A Shape Begins (4)
One, Two, Skip a few. (5)
Shape Spaces. (5)
10 sly piranhas
I Know Numbers            Shortest longest
I Know Shapes             # at the lake
Counting at market       Summertime Num

# Benny's Pennies

*Taught by Stephanie Sheffield*

In *Benny's Pennies*, written by Pat Brisson (1993), Benny McBride has five new pennies and wants to spend them on his family and his pets. He finds something special to buy for each—a rose for his mother, a cookie for his brother, a paper hat for his sister, a meaty bone for his dog, and a floppy fish for his cat. In this lesson, Stephanie Sheffield reads the book to both a first-grade and a kindergarten class and provides engaging activities to introduce the children to ways of counting and handling money.

## MATERIALS

plastic sandwich bags containing 1 quarter, 4 dimes, 6 nickels, 35 pennies, 1 bag per pair of students

coin stamps of a quarter, a dime, a nickel, and a penny

stamp pads

## Sharing the Book with a First-Grade Class

Stephanie read *Benny's Pennies* to her first graders after they had worked informally with money for a few months. They were eager to predict what would happen on each page. When Benny bought the rose, Nina spoke up, "It's for his mother!"

Eddie commented, "Now he has four pennies."

As Stephanie read each page, the class discussed who the gift was for and how much money Benny had left. She allowed the children to talk to one another as she read, and their discussion was animated and to the point. Although the book is simple, they enjoyed hearing it and retelling it.

The class acted out the story a few times, and then Stephanie could see that the children were ready for a new challenge. "Let's write our own version of the story," she suggested.

"We could call it *Jenny's Pennies*," Sharon said.

"OK," Stephanie responded. "What do we need to put into our story?"

The children decided they needed a main character (Jenny), some friends to give her advice about what to buy, a list of things to buy, and some money. The class spent some time talking about and recording words of advice from Jenny's friends, and chose its five favorite things on the list to include in the book:

something bright and delicious (Skittles candy)
something pretty that you can play with (a doll)
something plastic that holds water (a cup)
something colorful for writing (markers)
something with laces for running (sneakers)

Next Stephanie asked the children how much they thought Jenny should pay for each item. "The Skittles should cost a penny, like the things in the book," Timothy said.

"Then the doll should be twice as much," Eddie suggested. This puzzled some children, who weren't familiar with the phrase "twice as much."

"Can you explain for us what 'twice as much' means, Eddie?" Stephanie asked.

"I mean like double," he said. "Two is twice as much as one, so the doll should cost two cents. It's like when you roll doubles on dice." Stephanie watched the faces of the other students to see who registered a look of understanding and who still seemed to be unsure.

"How about another example?" Stephanie asked. "How much is twice as much as three? Tell the person next to you what you think."

After Cassie tried to explain to Mary why she thought it was six, she raised her hand and asked if she could use pennies from the class penny jar. Stephanie gave her a handful and she put out a row of three and another row of three under it. "There," she said, "I doubled it. Now you try, Mary." Cassie made a row of five pennies and Mary placed five pennies under it.

"Five and five is ten. Now I get it!" Mary said. Other students who noticed how Cassie had used the pennies came to the front of the room to get their own pennies from the penny jar.

After giving the children a few minutes to explore the idea of twice as much, Stephanie refocused the students' attention on their story. "Who can tell how much the cup should cost if we use Eddie's pattern of doubling?"

Maya raised her hand. "Two and two is four," she said. "That's double, so the cup is four cents," she said. Stephanie recorded *4 cents* on the board next to the description of the cup. She also recorded the prices of the Skittles and the doll. Kimberly suggested eight cents for the markers, the next item on the list, and Stephanie saw heads around the room nod in agreement.

The final price proved more difficult. "But you can't get eight on one die," Harlan said. He had used the dots on dice to add the other numbers. Next to him, Nina moved eight pennies into a row and used Harlan's pennies to make another row.

"It's sixteen!" he exclaimed.

Around the room, students pooled their pennies to verify the answer. When they were all satisfied, the class moved on.

(**Note:** Stephanie decided to continue with Eddie's doubling suggestion and use it as the basis for the rest of the lesson. The plan she had had in mind before Eddie suggested doubling was to ask the children to think of some sort of pattern the class might use for the prices of the items in its story. Stephanie had thought that perhaps a child would suggest that the amounts go up by fives, with the first costing five cents, the second ten cents, and so on. Or, she thought, a child might suggest that each item cost two cents more than the one before, or one cent more. Then students could figure out how much money was needed altogether. Stephanie thinks that when she does this lesson again, she'll try her original plan. If no student suggests a pattern, then she'll suggest one.)

"I've noticed something different about our story from the book we read," Stephanie said. "In *Benny's Pennies*, we knew from the beginning that Benny had five pennies, but in our story we don't know how many pennies Jenny will need to make all of her purchases. Do you think you could figure that out?"

Most of the students seemed confident about their ability to do this. Stephanie told them they could work in pairs or choose to work alone, and she distributed paper for them to record their solutions. "Remember to explain with words, numbers, or pictures how you figure out the answer," she reminded them.

Many students used pennies to solve the problem. Some drew circles to represent the pennies. Stephanie noticed that while most of the children were counting the pennies by ones, Alex and Conner were making groups of ten. Having children work on a problem like this allowed Stephanie to observe their approaches and informally assess their understanding.

When Stephanie called the class back together, she asked students to present their solutions. Ronnie and Timothy went first. They came up to the front of the room and showed their paper. Ronnie read,

"We drew the pennies and counted by twos. We had one left over and that made thirty-one cents."

Audrey and Harlan stood next to their desks for their presentation and pointed to the groups of 1, 2, 4, 8, and 16 pennies they had arranged. "We got thirty-one, too. We counted by ones," Audrey reported.

Alex and Conner had also started with groups of 1, 2, 4, 8, and 16. They explained how they then took the 2 pennies and put them with the 8 pennies to make 10 pennies. They made two more groups of 10 using the pennies from the group of 4 and the group of 16. One penny was left over.

Having children explain how they reason provides the kind of informal peer teaching that is valuable for helping children think about counting objects in different ways. The class agreed that Jenny needed thirty-one cents. It was the end of class, and Stephanie promised they would continue working on their book the next day.

For the next day, Stephanie prepared a plastic sandwich bag for each pair of students with one quarter, four dimes, six nickels, and thirty-five pennies in it. Stephanie thinks it's important for children to use real money to solve problems. Plastic money doesn't look, sound, or feel like real coins, and as adults we use all of those attributes to identify money. We can all tell when we reach into our pockets which coins we have, just by how they feel. We're familiar with the sounds coins make when they jingle together and can probably identify some by their sound. Children need opportunities to handle real money in order to develop that same familiarity.

Stephanie asked the class to think about different assortments of coins Jenny could use to have thirty-one cents to pay for all the things she bought. She then showed the children how they were to record their ideas. She gave each pair of students a sheet of paper and demonstrated how to use it.

"Fold it in half, then in half again the other way," she explained as she demonstrated. "How many boxes do you think your paper will have when you open it?" Some children predicted, and others folded and opened their papers to count.

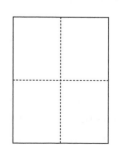

*Math and Literature, Grades K–1*

"Your problem is to think of four different ways Jenny might have a total of thirty-one cents to pay for her purchases," Stephanie said. "When you both agree that you have one way to make thirty-one cents, come to the table in the front. On the table are coin stamps and stamp pads. Record your answer in one box on your paper by stamping to show which coins you used. Then go back to your seat and find another way to make thirty-one cents."

The children were eager and interested in this problem. It was related to the *Jenny's Pennies* book they were making, and using real money and coin stamps was highly motivating. The stamps Stephanie had available showed both the fronts and backs of coins. Although the children were not as familiar with the stamps of the backs, they had the actual coins with them as they recorded their answers, so they just turned the coins over to make the match. (See Figure 1–1.)

Kimberly and Sharon were the first to fill up their four squares. They brought their paper to Stephanie, and she had them take turns

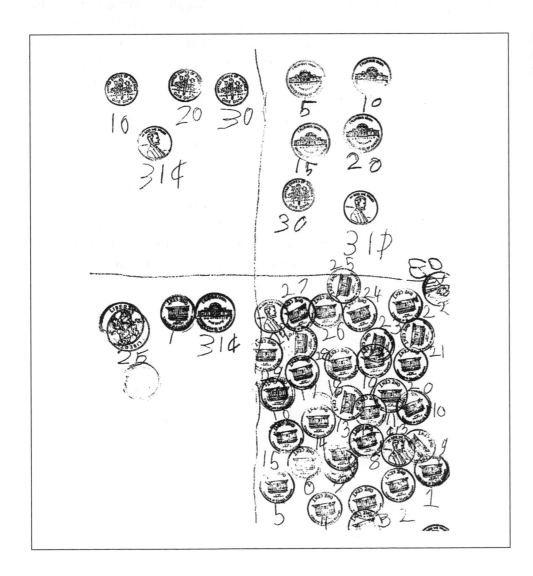

Figure 1–1: The students used coin stamps to record their answers.

counting the money they had stamped. This gave Stephanie the chance to assess informally what they had done and to see if they both understood their solutions. She watched to see how they counted the coins. Did they begin with the largest denomination or did they start randomly? Did they make the transition smoothly from counting by tens to counting by fives or did they hesitate? Did they point to each coin as they counted it or did they have another way to keep track of which ones they had already counted? When the girls finished counting, Stephanie asked if they could think of any other ways to make thirty-one cents with coins.

"Are there more?" Kimberly asked. "We filled up all the squares!"

"I know of at least one more way it can be done with the coins in your baggie," Stephanie told them. "If you find another way, turn your paper over and record it in one of the boxes on the back." They ran back to their seats to look for another solution. (See Figure 1–2.)

After each pair had found at least four solutions, Stephanie called the class together. "Let's share what we've found," Stephanie said. She let each pair of children choose one solution to share aloud. She asked them to tell the class how many of each coin they used to make thirty-one cents. Stephanie encouraged the others to listen carefully to see if they could identify the solution presented as the same as one of their own. If they did, they were to put a check in that box and try to find a different solution to share.

The first graders had difficulty comparing their solutions with the ones being described. If their own coins were placed in the box differently from the way someone else called them out, it was hard for them to identify the coins and keep track. But Stephanie thought it was good listening practice for them anyway.

The class was amazed at how many different solutions there were. As children presented, Stephanie recorded their solutions on the board as a way to keep track of them. After three pairs had reported, the chart looked like this:

| Quarters | Dimes | Nickels | Pennies |
|----------|-------|---------|---------|
| 0 | 3 | 0 | 1 |
| 1 | 0 | 1 | 1 |
| 0 | 1 | 4 | 1 |

"Hey, there's a pattern!" Timothy exclaimed. "There's always one in the Pennies column."

"That's because it's always thirty-*one* cents," Conner told him. Stephanie could see that what seemed obvious to Conner was a curious pattern to Timothy.

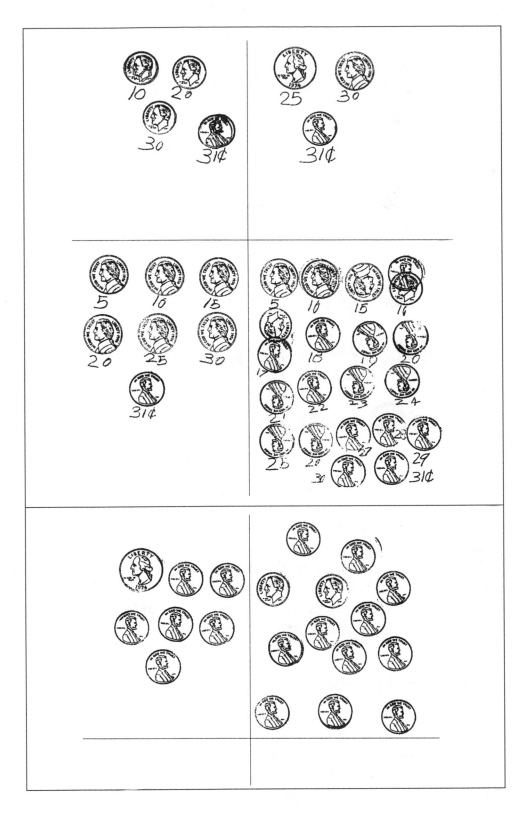

Figure 1–2: When Kimberly and Sharon learned that there were more than four solutions to the problem, they turned over their paper and found two more ways to show thirty-one cents.

"I did it with six pennies," Kimberly said, showing how she and Sharon had stamped one quarter and six pennies. Both Conner and Timothy looked surprised.

When the class left the problem, Stephanie had recorded eight different ways on the chart. Some students were still not convinced that

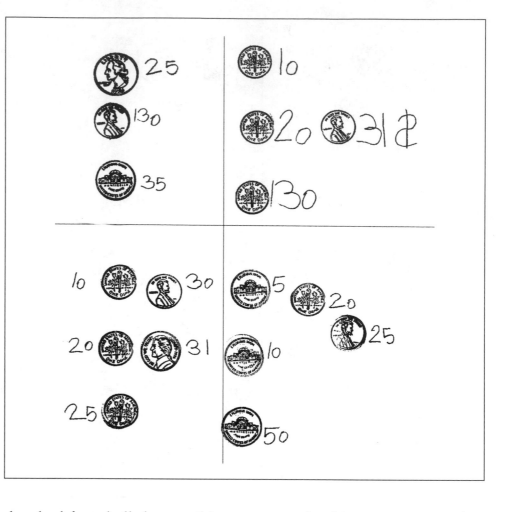

they had found all the possible ways to make thirty-one cents. (They hadn't; there are eighteen ways in all.) Stephanie left the bags of coins and the coin stamps in the math center for students to continue to explore. The class finished its work with *Benny's Pennies* by writing and illustrating a class book and sharing it with another class. (See Figure 1–3 for another student's work on this activity.)

## Sharing the Book with a Kindergarten Class

When Stephanie read this book to kindergartners, they'd already had some experience identifying coins. She showed the picture of Benny as he starts out in the morning. Covering up the part of the picture that shows his hand holding one penny, Stephanie said, "How many pennies does he have in this hand?"

"Four," Ruben answered.

"So how many pennies do you think are in his other hand?" Stephanie asked.

"One!" some students called out.

Stephanie stopped after she read the page where Benny asks for advice about what to buy.

"He should buy a candy cane," Julio suggested.

"Yeah, a candy cane," others agreed.

"What else could he buy?" Stephanie asked.

"A lollipop," Jennifer suggested.

"Some bubble gum," Vanessa offered.

"Let's see what he does buy," Stephanie said. She continued reading.

After Benny made his first purchase, Vanessa spoke up again. "Now he's only got four pennies," she said. She showed Stephanie four fingers. "But he's got one good thing, so it's still five."

After Benny bought the second item—the cookie—several children held up their hands to show Stephanie three fingers. They continued to show Stephanie their fingers as they counted down with the story.

When Stephanie read the book a second time, she asked the children to keep track of the numbers of pennies. At the beginning of the book, she asked how many pennies Benny had. The children each showed her five fingers.

"Show me on your other hand how many good things he has," Stephanie said. The students held up their other hands with no fingers showing.

With each page Stephanie read, the children each put down one finger on one hand and put up a finger on the other hand. With four fingers on one hand and one on the other, Kareem said, "It's still five showing."

"What do you mean, Kareem?" Stephanie asked.

"Four and one is five!" Kareem was confident about all the combinations of five.

Shontay, like some others, watched her friends before deciding if she had the correct number of fingers showing. Arturo and Yesinia just sat and enjoyed the book, without participating in the counting at all. This was fine with Stephanie. Children bring different things to mathematical experiences. Reading a book like *Benny's Pennies* can help some children reinforce their understanding while leading others to expand their awareness of numbers.

# The Button Box

*Taught by Bonnie Tank*

*The Button Box*, by Margarette S. Reid (1990), is a delightful invitation to the pleasures of a button collection. A little boy with a vivid imagination is fascinated and entertained by his grandmother's button collection. He imagines where the buttons came from and the clothes they once adorned. His grandmother plays sorting games with him and tells stories about what some of the buttons used to be. The book ends with a brief history of buttons. In this lesson, Bonnie Tank reads the book to a kindergarten class and engages the children in several days of activities in which they sort, count, describe, and compare buttons.

## MATERIALS

**several buttons for the class button box,** for children who don't bring a button from home

**a container for the class button collection**

**chart paper,** 1 sheet

**12-by-18-inch newsprint,** 1 sheet per pair of students

**1 large spoon that can hold 10–15 buttons**

## Day 1

Bonnie gathered the kindergarten children to read *The Button Box* to them. The boy in the story sorts the buttons in several ways, first picking the ones with flowers painted on them, then looking for sparkly buttons that he pretends are jewels, and next looking for buttons covered with fabric. He continues playing with the buttons, finding metal ones, buttons made of leather, small buttons that once were on shoes, shiny buttons, pearly ones, and buttons with four holes, two holes, and no holes at all. He describes the game he sometimes plays with his grandma—each takes a button and then they compare how their buttons are alike and different. The book continues with his grandma telling him stories about different buttons and where they came from.

After reading the story, Bonnie read the last page, which gives some history about buttons. Then she asked, "Who has a button collection at home?" Many children raised their hands.

"Can anyone describe the container that holds your buttons?" Bonnie then asked.

"We have a button box," Cynthia said, "but it's like a rectangle, not a circle like the one in the book."

"Our buttons are in a can," Paul said. "It's taller than the one in the book."

Other children also described their containers. Bonnie suspected that several of the children described imaginary button boxes that had lids with hinges and locks and keys. It was clear that some of the children thought of button collections as real treasures.

"Is anybody wearing buttons today?" Bonnie asked.

Seven children were wearing buttons, and Bonnie asked them to come to the front of the class. The class counted how many buttons each child had. Devin noticed that four people had two buttons. Charles commented that Emma had more buttons than anyone else.

After the seven children returned to their seats, Bonnie told the students they were going to start a class button collection. She asked that each child bring one button to school. To help them remember, and to give parents information, Bonnie sent home the following note along with an envelope for the button with each child:

*Dear Parents,*

*After reading and discussing Margarette S. Reid's book* The Button Box *with the class, the children have become interested and curious about buttons. I've asked each to bring a button to school for our class button collection. We will be doing a variety of math activities that will engage the children in sorting, comparing, and counting buttons. Please send a button you no longer need.*

*Thank you.*

## Day 2

Bonnie brought extra buttons to add to the class collection so that any child who didn't bring a button could still participate. To begin the class exploration of buttons, Bonnie had the children sit in a circle on the rug. "Put your button on the floor in front of you so that everyone can see it," Bonnie instructed. Then she said, "I wonder if any of our buttons are the same."

The children noticed that several students had brought white buttons. Upon closer inspection, they noticed differences—some had two holes and some had four, some were small and some were big. The children also made other observations—that Jenny had brought a button shaped like a heart, for example, and that Georgia's button was shiny and looked like a flower.

Bonnie then organized the children into pairs to compare their buttons. She chose Lea for a partner and modeled for the children what they were to do. Bonnie made an observation. "My button is red and Lea's is green," she said. "Now you tell something that you notice about how our buttons are the same or different," she instructed Lea.

Lea thought for a moment and then said, "Mine has two holes and yours has four."

"With your partner," Bonnie said, "take turns telling something that is the same or different about your buttons." After giving them a few minutes to compare buttons in pairs, Bonnie had a class discussion in which children reported what they had noticed about their buttons.

Bonnie collected the buttons by playing a game. She gave directions such as "Button, button, who has a button that's not white?" and "Button, button, who has a button that's round?" When a description fit, children deposited their buttons in the cookie tin that one of the parents had donated. Bonnie added the buttons she had brought.

## Day 3

The following day, Bonnie taped a sheet of chart paper on the front board and had the class gather on the rug. She taped two buttons next to each other at the top of the chart.

"Who can tell something that's either the same or different about these two buttons?" Bonnie asked. As the children provided information, Bonnie recorded what they said on the chart:

> *One button looks like butterscotch.*
> *One is big and one is little.*
> *One has two holes and one has four.*
> *The buttons are different colors.*
> *One is white and one is orange.*
> *The buttons are both round.*

*The white one looks like a plate.*
*They both have a bump. One bump is outside and one is inside.*
*One is thick and one is not.*
*One is wide and one is not.*

## Day 4

The next day, Bonnie again had the children sit in a circle on the rug. She had a sheet of 12-by-18-inch newsprint, the button box, crayons, and a spoon to demonstrate the activity they would do that day. "You and your partner will use one sheet of paper," Bonnie began. "First you'll fold your paper in half and write your names." Bonnie demonstrated how to fold the paper and, with Weslie as her partner, showed how they would write their names on different halves of the paper.

"Then I'll come around and put a spoonful of buttons on your paper," Bonnie continued. Using a large serving spoon, she put a spoonful on the sheet of paper she shared with Weslie, trying to keep the number of buttons between ten and fifteen.

"Your job is to sort the buttons in different ways," Bonnie said. "You tell one thing about the buttons, and then sort them into two sets. Let's try it with the buttons Weslie and I have. Who notices one thing about some of the buttons?"

"Some are white," Georgia said.

"On one half of the paper," Bonnie said, "put the buttons that are white. The rest go on the other side." Several of the children sitting nearby helped demonstrate. Then Bonnie asked the children

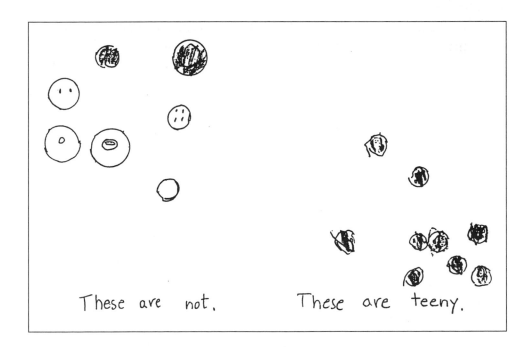

Figure 2–1: Donna and Kyle sorted their buttons by size.

Figure 2–2: Rory and Lisa
sorted their buttons into
three groups.

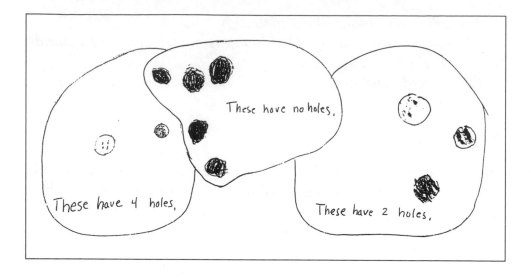

for other ways to sort the buttons, and they did so several more times.

"Finally," Bonnie said, "you and your partner have to record one of the ways you sorted." Weslie said she wanted to sort their buttons by round and not round and quickly sorted them on the paper. Bonnie then showed the children how to trace the buttons and color them in on the paper. On one half of the paper, she wrote: *These are round*; on the other half, she wrote: *These are not round.*

"I'll help you write when you know what you want to say," she told the class. The children returned to the tables to work. They sorted their buttons in several ways: *These are teeny. These are not.* (See Figure 2–1.) *These are colored buttons. These are white buttons.*

Some children sorted the buttons into more than two groups: *These have 4 holes. These have no holes. These have 2 holes.* (See Figure 2–2.)

The children's interest in buttons was evident, and Bonnie planned to continue the exploration with further activities.

# Cats Add Up!

*Taught by Leyani von Rotz*

Dianne Ochiltree's book *Cats Add Up!* (1998) is about a girl who has one cat but then adopts more, even though her mother says over and over again that one cat is just the right number to have. When ten cats are in the house, and the girl's mother is overcome with sneezing and wheezing, the girl gives nine of the cats to different neighbors. In this lesson, Leyani von Rotz uses the story to engage first graders in thinking about addition as more and more cats arrive; to encourage them to figure how many eyes, ears, and paws there are for ten cats; and to give them experience with subtraction as the cats are adopted by others.

**MATERIALS**

Leyani gathered the first graders on the rug to hear her read aloud *Cats Add Up!* She showed the children the cover of the book.

"She has a lot of cats," Tyrone said, commenting on the cover illustration, which shows a girl sitting on the floor, surrounded by cats.

"I have a cat," Paulo shared.

"Me, too," said Ramya, David, Vincent, and Farrell.

"My grandma has two cats," Clauda added.

"The title of this book is *Cats Add Up!*" Leyani told the children. "Listen as I read and you'll find out about how the girl got so many cats."

Leyani opened the book to the first spread, which shows the girl outside playing with her cat, Maxie, while her mother is hanging the wash out to dry. "One is just the right number of cats for us," her mother says, a comment that she repeats throughout the book.

But then five homeless kittens appear in a box at the front door. Even though Mama protests that six cats are five too many, the girl names the cats and begins to play with them. Next a neighbor who is moving to a place that doesn't allow pets delivers his two cats to the girl, and Mama now complains that eight cats are seven too many. The next day the girl brings home from school a stray cat that has hopped into her backpack, making nine cats, and when her mother comes into the front door with the groceries, another cat scoots in behind her. Now there are ten cats.

Mama sighs and begins to fix dinner, watched by twenty cat eyes. Ten tails scurry about, twenty ears perk up when a dog barks, and forty paws scratch Mama's new chair. Pretty soon, Mama begins to sneeze and wheeze, and the girl knows that they can't keep all ten cats. The next day she posts signs everywhere: Free Cats. Different neighbors adopt them; first Mrs. Minnow takes one, then the new neighbor takes two, and so on until the girl and Mama are home alone with just Maxie. But then there is a surprise—Maxie has four kittens!

The children giggled at the end of the story. Then they shared what they liked about the story.

"I liked how the cat ran into the house when Mama was coming in with the groceries," Hallie said.

"I liked how they all played in the house when Mama was cooking," Jamila added.

"Did she get to keep the little kittens at the end?" Natalie wanted to know, concerned.

Leyani said, "Let me read the end of the story again." She reread the last page in the book: "Maxie had four kittens! And what do you think Mama said about *that*?" Then she asked Natalie, "What do you think?"

"I think she kept them," Natalie said, nodding.

"But maybe Mama sneezed again," Elana said, worried about the mother.

"I hope she got to keep them," Travis said.

Leyani then said, "I'm going to read the book again now. And this time I'm going to keep track of the cats on the board by writing a number sentence each time more cats arrive."

When the five kittens were left at the front door, Leyani asked, "Who has an idea about a number sentence I might write?"

Jamila suggested, "Five plus one equals six." Leyani recorded on the board:

$$5 + 1 = 6$$

Hallie said, "It should be one plus five because the big cat was there first and then came the kittens." Leyani recorded Hallie's idea on the board underneath Jamila's:

$$5 + 1 = 6$$
$$1 + 5 = 6$$

Students commented on the two sentences. "They're both sort of right," David said.

"But I think that Hallie is right, the big cat comes first," Clauda said.

Leyani didn't resolve the question but instead continued with the story. On the next page, when two more cats arrived, Paulo suggested, "Two plus five plus one."

As Leyani recorded on the board, Vincent called out, excitedly, "That's eight!" Leyani completed the number sentence:

$$2 + 5 + 1 = 8$$

"I know another way to make eight," Jerilyn commented. "Four plus four makes eight." Even though it didn't relate to the story, Leyani recorded Jerilyn's idea, writing it to the side of the list:

$$4 + 4 = 8$$

By the time there were ten cats in the story, Leyani had recorded the following number sentences in the list:

$$5 + 1 = 6$$
$$1 + 5 = 6$$
$$2 + 5 + 1 = 8$$
$$1 + 2 + 5 + 1 = 9$$
$$1 + 2 + 5 + 1 + 1 = 10$$

Underneath the sentence that Jerilyn had suggested, written to the side of the list, Leyani wrote Anna's suggestion for a number sentence that was true but that also didn't relate to the story—$5 + 5 = 10$.

Leyani stopped reading at this point in the story and gave the students directions for an assignment they were to do individually. She said, "I'd like you to pick a number sentence from the board and show what it means by drawing on your paper. You can draw cats, but if you don't want to draw cats, what else could you draw?"

"Circles," Peter suggested.

"Lines," Cameron suggested.

"Just shapes," Tyrone suggested.

Before dismissing the children from the rug to go to their seats and begin working, Leyani said, "Think quietly in your heads about the number sentence you'll choose and what you're going to draw to show the cats. When you've decided, raise your hand." As children raised their hands, Leyani dismissed them. She didn't have them announce their choices. Sometimes when one child makes a choice, the others follow along rather than make their own decisions. Leyani wanted to avoid this happening as it had in the past.

The children went to work enthusiastically, some carefully drawing cats and others using circles, squares, triangles, hearts, or other shapes to represent them. Some children wanted to color their pictures; others chose to use their time to illustrate another number sentence. The children's papers helped Leyani assess their ability to interpret number sentences. (See Figures 3–1 through 3–5.)

Figure 3–1: Cameron used different-colored crayons to differentiate the addends in the number sentence.

Figure 3–2: Farrell drew cats to illustrate 5 + 5 = 10, the number sentence that Anna had suggested.

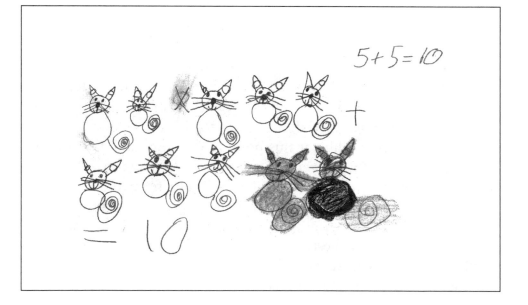

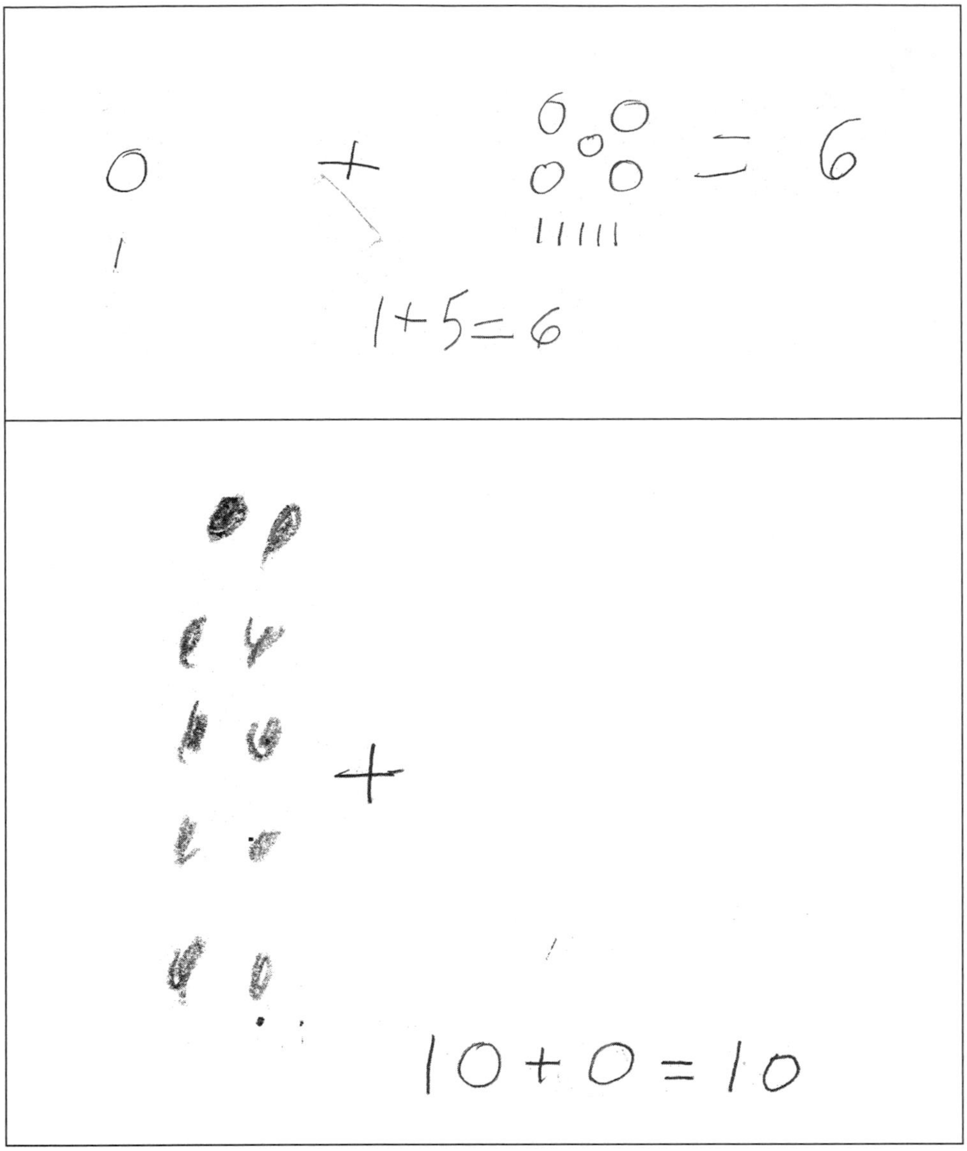

0    +    ○ ○ ○
          ○   ○ ○    = 6

1                |||||

1 + 5 = 6

10 + 0 = 10

Figure 3–3: Vincent illustrated the number sentence 1 + 5 = 6 with dots in a domino pattern and with tally marks.

5 + 1 = 6

Figure 3–4: Anna drew cats to illustrate 5 + 1 = 6, coloring in the last cat to show that it represented the 1 in the number sentence.

Figure 3–5: Jerilyn decided to illustrate a collection of number sentences, drawing circles to represent the addends. She started with 7 + 3 = 10, but then Leyani asked her to focus on the number sentences from the story.

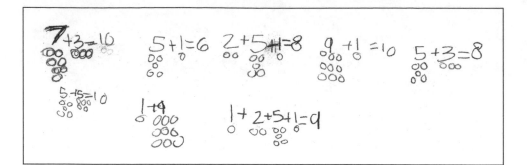

*Math and Literature, Grades K–1*

# Inch by Inch

## *Taught by Leyani von Rotz*

Illustrated with vibrant cutouts on white backgrounds, Leo Lionni's *Inch by Inch* (1995) tells the story of an inchworm able to measure anything who proves it by measuring a robin's tail, a flamingo's neck, a toucan's beak, a heron's legs, a pheasant's tail, and the entire length of a hummingbird. When confronted with the challenge of either measuring a nightingale's song or being eaten, the inchworm creatively solves his problem. In this lesson, Leyani von Rotz reads the book to a kindergarten class and uses it as the springboard for an introductory experience with inches and linear measurement.

### MATERIALS

**1-inch color tiles,** at least 10 per student

After setting out a basket of tiles at each table, Leyani gathered the kindergarten children on the rug and showed them the cover of *Inch by Inch*. Several children had comments.

"I see flowers there, there, and there," Daniela said, pointing to the three flowers she noticed on the cover illustration.

"I see grass," Jorge said.

"That one has stripes," Hallie said, pointing to one of the blades of grass.

"And there are leaves," Raul added.

Christian jumped up and said excitedly, "Look, there's a worm!" He had noticed the worm crawling up to the top of one of the blades of grass.

"And there's a circle," Melody said, referring to the Caldecott Honor Book award on the cover.

Leyani explained, "This isn't something that the artist drew. It's a special award the artist received for his wonderful illustrations in this book." Leyani then read the title to the children and said, "The worm on the cover is an inchworm and this is a story about his adventures."

Leyani opened the book to the first spread and read about the hungry robin who is about to eat the inchworm. "Do you see the inchworm?" she asked the children, pointing to the inchworm sitting on a twig. The children nodded. They sat quietly, worrying about the inchworm they had just met.

The next page reveals that the inchworm talks his way out of being eaten by convincing the robin that he is useful. "I measure things," the inchworm says. The robin demands that the inchworm measure his tail, and the following spread shows him doing so, inching down the tail and counting, "One, two, three, four, five inches."

The robin is so pleased that, with the inchworm on his back, he flies to where other birds need to be measured. The next five spreads show the inchworm measuring the neck of a flamingo, the beak of a toucan, the legs of a heron, the tail of a pheasant, and the length of a hummingbird.

But when the inchworm meets the nightingale, the nightingale presents him with an unusual challenge: "Measure my song or I'll eat you for breakfast." The inchworm is stumped at first. He knows how to measure things, but not songs. Then he has an idea. He asks the nightingale to start singing and, as the nightingale sings, the inchworm measures away through the grass, inch by inch, until he is safely out of sight.

"He got away," Bobby said.

"He was smart," Daniela added. "He let the bird sing and then he went into the grass."

Leyani then showed the children a 1-inch color tile. "Each side of this tile is one inch long," she said. "The inchworm is called an inchworm because it's one inch long." Leyani put down the tile and held up her two index fingers so that they were about an inch apart. "Hold up your fingers so that they are about one inch apart," she said to the children. They all did so and Leyani scanned to be sure that their fingers were close to being an inch apart.

Then Leyani held her fingers so that they were about two feet apart. "Am I showing one inch now?" she asked. Most of the children shook their heads "no," but a few nodded.

Leyani said, "Now the distance between my fingers is much, much more than one inch. Here's what one inch looks like." Leyani moved her fingers together again to show 1 inch. The children imitated her.

Leyani then picked up the color tile and held one of its edges to her thumb, showing the children that the distance from the tip of her thumb to the knuckle was just about 1 inch. "This part of my thumb measures just about one inch," she said. Then she held her thumb out straight. "But my whole thumb is longer than one inch. I think that if the inchworm measured my thumb, he would find out that it's about two inches long. I can pretend that this tile is the inchworm and measure." She again placed the tile so an edge began at the tip of her thumb and then moved it to measure, saying as she did this, "My thumb is one inch from the tip to here, so then I'll move it down to the next space, and there's room for another inch. Yes, my thumb is just about two inches long, maybe a little longer."

"What about my nose?" she continued. "What if the inchworm measured my nose? Is my nose the same length as the color tile? Is it one inch? Or is it more than one inch or less than one inch?" Leyani placed the color tile so one end of a side was at the tip of her nose. She turned sideways so the children could compare the lengths of the tile and her nose. The children giggled.

"Your nose is bigger," Raul said.

"Maybe it's two," Frannie said.

"Two what?" Leyani asked.

"Two of those," Frannie said, pointing to the tile.

"Oh, you mean two inches?" Leyani asked. Frannie nodded.

Leyani then opened the book to the spread that showed the inchworm measuring the toucan's beak. She chose not to show the page where the inchworm measured the robin's tail because that's the only page that tells the measurement the inchworm got—5 inches—but the robin's tail isn't nearly that long in the book. She also chose not to use the page with the flamingo because the neck is long and curvy. On the page with the toucan, the beak is fairly straight and the inchworm in the illustration is just about exactly 1 inch.

Leyani held the color tile up to the inchworm in the illustration and said, "See, the inchworm is just about one inch long. How many inches do you think he measured on the toucan's beak, starting at the green part and going to the tip?" The children's predictions ranged from 2 to 10 inches. Hearing from individual students gave Leyani a way to assess which children understood the idea of measuring in inches and could give a reasonable estimate.

"Let's find out," Leyani said. She laid the book flat on the rug and then placed a color tile at one end of the toucan's beak. "I'm going to use more color tiles and put them down one right next to the other with no spaces in between," Leyani explained. "Then we can see how many inches long the beak is. You count as I put the tiles down." As the children counted, Leyani placed nine tiles.

"So the toucan's beak is nine inches long," Leyani said. "Show me again with your fingers how long one inch is." As the children held up their fingers, Leyani scanned and saw that they all did this correctly. "Now hold your fingers apart to show how long the toucan's beak is," Leyani said and then added, "So now your fingers are nine inches apart."

Next Leyani showed them the page with the hummingbird. "How long do you think the hummingbird is?" she asked.

"All the way to the end of his nose?" Purna wanted to know.

Leyani responded, "Yes, from the end of his tail feathers to the tip of his beak. Hold up your fingers to show how long you think the hummingbird is." The children did this, some more successfully than others.

"How many inches long do you think the hummingbird is?" Leyani asked again. The answers ranged from 2 to 7 inches. As she had done with the toucan's beak, Leyani placed the book on the rug and modeled how to measure with color tiles.

"It's four inches," Hallie announced after the children had counted.

Leyani then introduced the activity the children would do independently. "Now you'll have the chance to measure how many inches long some things are. You'll use the color tiles, just as I did. But first, you have to decide what you'll measure."

Leyani then gave an example to model for the children what they might do. She said, "I think I'll measure how many inches long the title of the book is." She placed the book on the rug with the cover facing up and placed a color tile just underneath the beginning of the title, *Inch by Inch*. "I'll measure how many tiles it takes to get to the end of the title," she continued. "But I have to be careful to place the tiles without leaving any spaces in between them." Leyani placed the tiles as the children counted. When she was done, she said, "So the title is five inches long."

To show the children how they were to record, Leyani took a piece of paper, placed it over the title on the cover, and traced the letters. Then she traced the row of five color tiles that she had placed to measure the length of the title. Finally she wrote the numeral *5*.

"You don't have to measure something on the book," Leyani said. "You could measure a pencil, or a piece of chalk, or anything else in the room. But whatever you pick shouldn't be longer than this edge of the book." Leyani ran her finger up and down the spine of the book to show the children what she meant. Keeping the objects small made it possible for children to trace them on paper and kept the counting within their grasp.

"Look around the room and see what you could measure," she said and then called on children for their ideas. The children burst out with ideas. "A block." "My shoe." "A piece of paper." "My finger." "The pencil cup."

Leyani quieted them and said, "When you tell me your idea, I'll give you a piece of paper. There are color tiles on all of the tables. Take what you are measuring and trace it on your paper. Then measure how many inches long it is. And then write down the number that tells how many tiles you used." As the children gave their ideas, Leyani gave them a sheet of paper and dismissed them from the rug.

As she circulated, Leyani noticed that some children were clear about the task. Danny, for example, traced one of the blocks from the block corner and carefully placed color tiles to measure it. Then he drew the tiles, and even though he didn't show them on his paper placed side by side, he had measured correctly and wrote *11* on his paper, inside the block he had traced. (See Figure 4–1.)

Two children, Frannie and Daniela, traced and measured their feet. "Hey," Frannie said when she noticed that her measurement of 8 inches was less than Daniela's measurement of 14. But Daniela pointed out that she had measured around her foot, and Frannie, who had measured the length of her foot, was satisfied.

Some children, however, had difficulty. Hallie, for example, was measuring a pencil and didn't line the tiles up next to one another but placed them randomly alongside the pencil. (Although Hallie had responded with confidence when Leyani had measured the

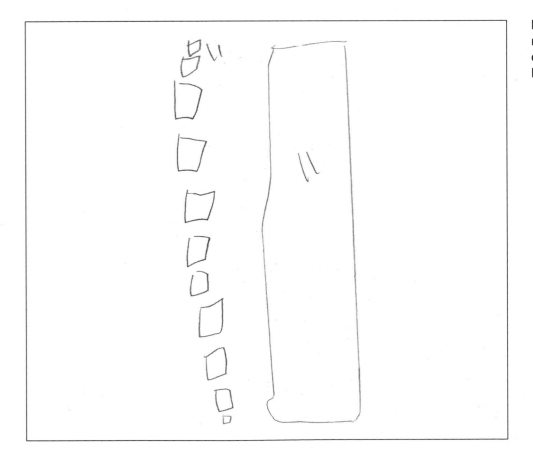

Figure 4–1: Danny correctly measured the block he chose, but he didn't draw his tiles accurately.

hummingbird, her response hid her lack of understanding about how to measure correctly.) Gwen traced a block and then covered the shape with tiles instead of measuring its length. However, she was satisfied with her effort, clearly more interested in the task she had chosen than in what Leyani had assigned. And Purna, not sure what to do, filled her paper with numbers. Leyani tried steering children who weren't doing the assignment as she had explained, but she didn't push them.

She knew that they would have many more measurement opportunities during the year.

A colleague observing the lesson asked Leyani if using interlocking cubes would be easier for the children to measure with, especially those who were doing what Hallie was and not placing tiles next to one another. Leyani's replied that she chose the tiles because their sides measured exactly 1 inch and, therefore, gave children experience with this standard measure of length. Leyani also explained that lining up the tiles to measure didn't offer the distraction of snapping cubes together and that the tiles were better than interlocking cubes for measuring curved lines. (Figures 4–2 through 4–5 show how some other students recorded their work.)

Figure 4–2: Melody traced her foot and used nine tiles to measure its, length. Although she correctly recorded the number 9, she drew only seven tiles, spending more of her time drawing the laces on her shoe.

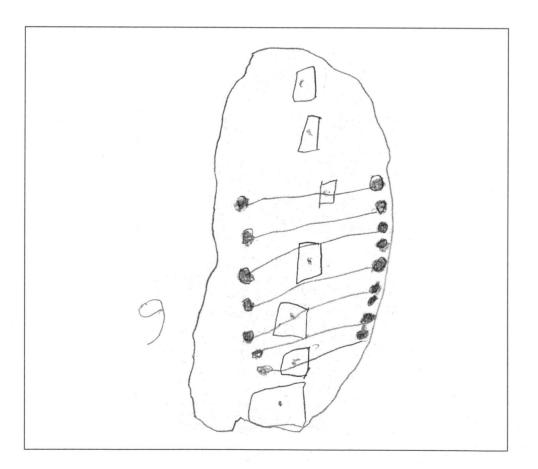

*Math and Literature, Grades K–1*

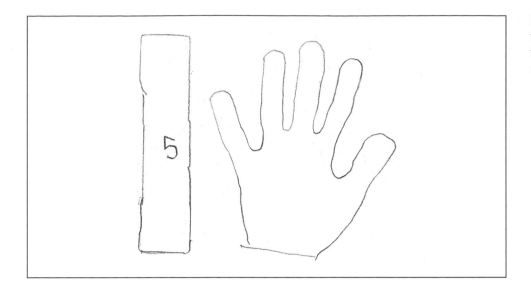

Figure 4–3: Raul carefully traced his hand and the train of five tiles he made to measure it.

Figure 4–4: Manny had time to measure the length of his hand and the length of a pencil. He was excited to find out that they were the same length, both 6 inches.

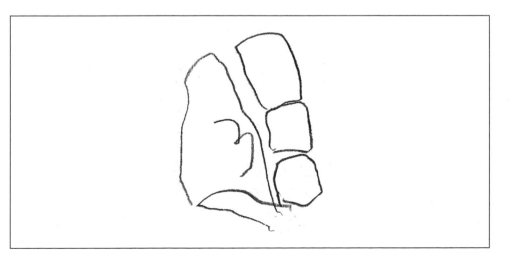

Figure 4–5: Jorge traced and measured his finger.

# Let's Go Visiting

*Taught by Leyani von Rotz*

*Let's Go Visiting*, by Sue Williams (1998), begins with a child suggesting to his dog that they go visiting. First they visit a brown foal, eager to play. The foal comes with them as they then visit two red calves, also eager to play. They then visit three black kittens, four pink piglets, five green ducklings, and finally six yellow puppies, with all of the animals joining them on the journey. The book ends with the child and all of the animals taking a nap in the hay. For this lesson, after introducing the book to a class of first graders, Leyani von Rotz has students solve the problem of figuring out how many animals the child and his dog visited.

## MATERIALS

Leyani gathered the first graders on the rug to read the book aloud to them. "The title of this book is *Let's Go Visiting*," she told the children. Leyani opened the book to the first page and read, "Let's go visiting. What do you say?"

"That's like my dog," Anna said, pointing to the golden retriever in the illustration.

"He has funny pants," Travis said, commenting on the boy's green pants covered with yellow circles.

Leyani turned the page and finished the rhyme, "One brown foal is ready to play." The illustration on that page shows the boy laughing, tickled by the young horse licking his face.

"What's a foal?" Leyani asked the children.

"It's a baby horse," Vincent said matter-of-factly.

The next page shows the foal joining the boy and his dog as they continue going visiting. They come upon two red calves, also ready to play.

"And what are calves?" Leyani asked.

"They look like cows," Jamila said.

"But they're different colors," Pablo added.

"They're baby cows!" David exclaimed.

Leyani turned the next page to show the calves joining the boy, his dog, and the foal as they continued. The following page shows them visiting three black kittens, and the children joined in as Leyani finished the text about them being "ready to play."

"They're all babies," Jerilyn said. "The kittens are baby cats."

"How many black kittens did they visit?" Leyani asked.

"Three," the children chorused.

"And how many animals do you think they'll visit next?" Leyani asked.

"Four," the students answered.

"I think they'll be babies, too," Ramya said.

"Let's see," Leyani said. She turned the page and read the repeating text, "Let's go visiting. What do you say?"

When she turned the page, several children called out, "Baby pigs." Leyani confirmed that they were visiting four pink piglets.

"They're playing in the mud," Clauda said.

Leyani said, "So they visited one foal, two calves, three kittens, and four piglets. How many will come next?"

"Five," the children chorused.

Leyani turned the page and said, "Read along with me." She pointed to the text. Some of the children read along, remembering the repeating line.

When she turned the page, Tyrone said, "We were right. There are five duckies."

"Yes," Leyani said. "And what color are the ducklings?"

"Green," the children responded. Leyani encouraged the children to read the text along with her about the five green ducklings being ready to play.

"Six come next," Farrell said, anticipating Leyani's next question. She clapped when Leyani read that six yellow puppies were ready to play.

"They're the babies of the big dog," Hallie said.

After finishing reading the book, Leyani asked the children to recall the animals in the book. "What was the first animal they visited?" she asked.

"A baby horse," Natalie answered. Leyani nodded, showed the children the page in the book with the foal, and then wrote on the board, reading to the class as she wrote:

*1 brown foal (baby horse)*

"And then what did they visit?" Leyani asked. As the children reported, she turned to the page in the book to verify their idea and then she recorded on the board. Finally she had listed all of the names of the baby animals and their adult counterparts.

*1 brown foal (baby horse)*
*2 red calves (baby cows)*
*3 black kittens (baby cats)*
*4 pink piglets (baby pigs)*
*5 green ducklings (baby ducks)*
*6 yellow puppies (baby dogs)*

"Here's a problem for you to solve," Leyani then said. "How many animals did the boy and his dog visit altogether? They visited one foal, two calves, three kittens, four piglets, five ducklings, and six puppies. How many animals did they visit in all?" A few children raised their hands to answer, but Leyani didn't call on them. Instead, she gave them directions about what they were to do.

"I'm going to give each of you a sheet of paper to use to figure out the number that's the answer to the problem," Leyani explained. "You can draw pictures of the animals or draw other shapes to show them. Use pictures, numbers, and words to help you solve the problem."

The children were eager to get started, but before giving them paper and dismissing them from the rug, Leyani asked, "Who can tell what the problem is that you're going to solve? Raise your hand if you can explain the problem."

Only a few children were willing to explain. Leyani did what she typically does in instances like this. "Turn and talk with your partner," she said. In this case, she gave more specific directions. "Take turns. First one of you tells the problem, and then the other has a chance." The room broke out into conversation. Farrell didn't have a partner, so Leyani told her the problem and then had her repeat it back. When Leyani called the children back to attention, she called on several children to share their ideas.

"We have to figure out how many baby animals they went to visit," Jamila said.

"We can draw pictures of them," Travis said, always interested in drawing.

"Or we can draw shapes if we don't want to draw the animals," Ramya said.

*Math and Literature, Grades K–1*

"We have to figure out the number," Anna added.

Leyani distributed the paper to the children, one by one, and dismissed them to return to their desks and begin working. Then Leyani circulated, helping the children keep on task, answering questions as needed, and talking with the children about their work.

The children approached the problem in different ways. Some focused on drawing the animals. Others represented them with dots, squares, hearts, or other shapes. Some children wrote the names of the animals and others didn't. Some wrote addition sentences. All solved the problem by counting. (See Figures 5–1 through 5–4.)

As is typical when children work on assignments, some worked more quickly than others. Leyani offered an extension problem to each of four students who completed the assignment early. She asked, "What if they kept on visiting animals so that they next met seven, then eight, then nine, and finally ten animals? Then how many animals would they have visited in all?" Of the children who tackled this challenge, three of the students arrived at the correct answer of fifty-five and one got the incorrect answer of fifty-one. One child, Jose, extended the problem for himself so that the characters also visited eleven, twelve, and thirteen animals. He counted carefully but arrived at the answer of nintey-six instead of ninety-one. (See Figures 5–5 through 5–7.)

Figure 5–1: Travis first became engrossed in drawing the animals but then got tired and reverted to using circles to represent them.

Figure 5–2: Elana drew hearts to represent the animals, using crayons in the colors that were in the story. She was upset that she drew one too many green hearts for the ducklings but was satisfied when Leyani told her she could just cross out the extra heart.

Figure 5–3: Paulo wrote the names of the adult animals and drew circles to represent them, coloring them in the colors from the story.

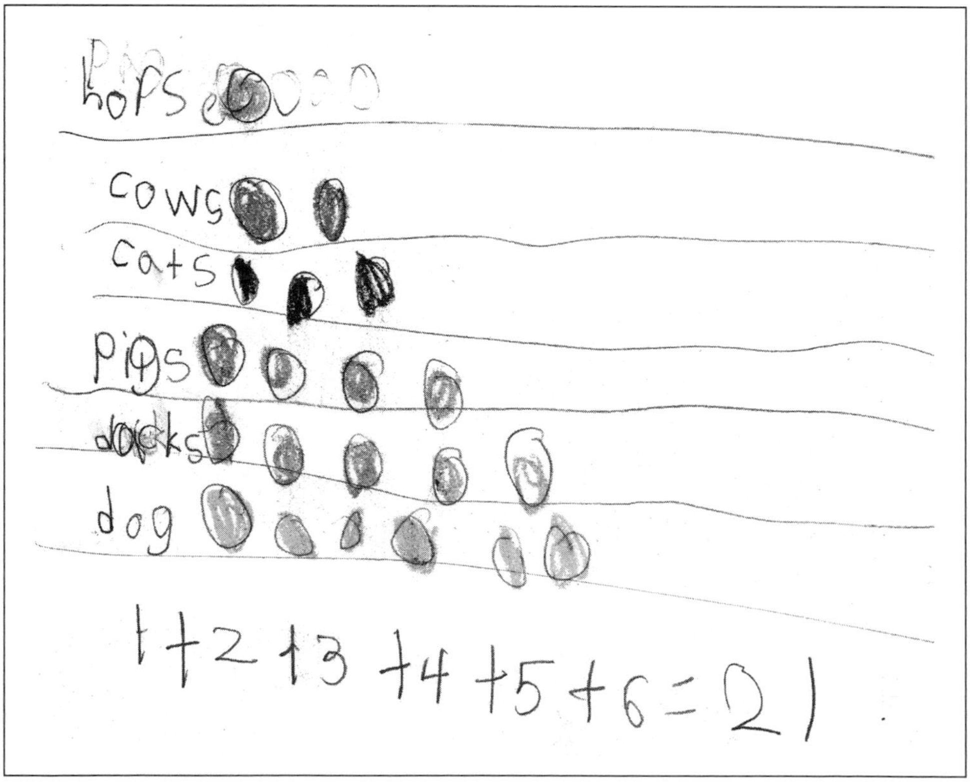

*Math and Literature, Grades K–1*

Figure 5–4: Jerilyn carefully copied from the board the names of the baby animals and adult animals. She used hearts in the correct colors to represent them, counted to get the answer, and also wrote an addition sentence.

1 bown foal ( baby horse.
2 red calves (baby cows)
3 black Kittens (baby cats
4 pink pigletts (baby pigs)
5 green ducklings ( baby ducks)
6 yellow puppies (baby dogs)
1+2+3+4+5+6=21

Figure 5–5: Jamila tried the challenge of extending the story up to visiting ten animals. She counted carefully, keeping track by writing the numbers in the shapes she drew. Her answer and number sentence were correct.

thar was 55 anmls!
20+20+10+5=55

Figure 5–6: For the extension problem, Cynthia drew triangles to represent the animals and then numbered them. However, she made an error in the last row, resulting in the incorrect answer of fifty-one instead of fifty-five.

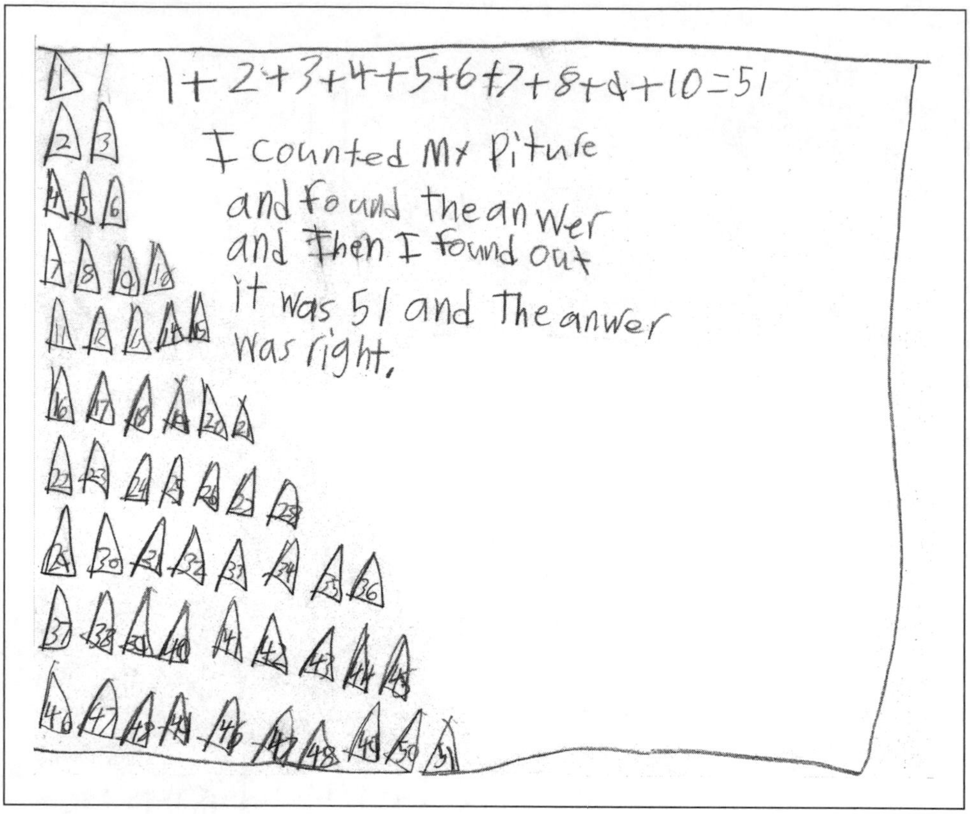

$1 + 2 + 3 + 4 + 5 + 6 + 7 + 8 + 9 + 10 = 51$

I counted my piture and found the anwer and then I found out it was 51 and the anwer was right.

Figure 5–7: Jose gave himself the harder challenge of adding the numbers from one to thirteen. He worked carefully and methodically but miscounted to get the answer of ninety-six instead of ninety-one.

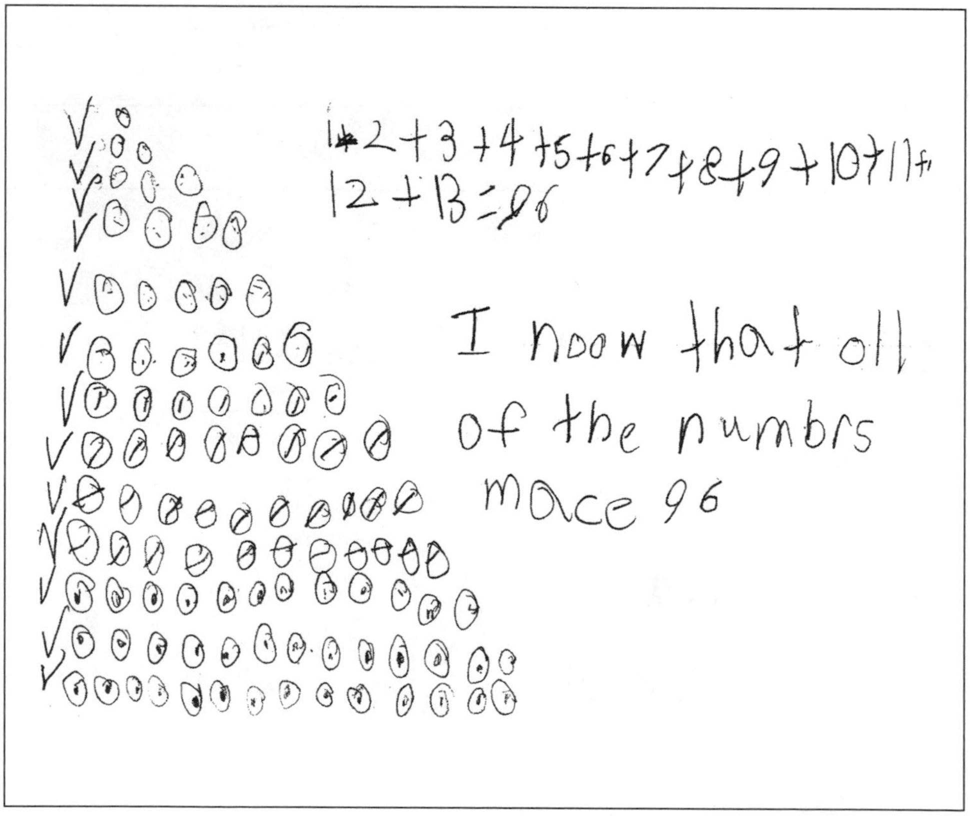

$1 + 2 + 3 + 4 + 5 + 6 + 7 + 8 + 9 + 10 + 11 +$
$12 + 13 = 86$

I noow that oll of the numbrs mace 96

# The Napping House

*Taught by Stephanie Sheffield*

*The Napping House*, by Audrey Wood (1984), is a beautifully illustrated book about a house full of napping inhabitants. The story begins with a granny snoring away on a dark and rainy day. One by one, she is joined in bed by a dreaming child, a dozing dog, a snoozing cat, a slumbering mouse, and finally, a wakeful flea. This last arrival begins a chain reaction that results in the whole group awakening just as the rain stops and the sun comes out. In this lesson, Stephanie Sheffield reads the book to a first-grade class and engages the children in a numerical problem-solving experience for which there are multiple answers.

## MATERIALS

$8\frac{1}{2}$-by-11-inch paper, 1 sheet per student

12-by-18-inch construction paper, 1 sheet per student

As soon as Stephanie put the big book version of *The Napping House* on the easel, she heard exclamations of recognition from the first graders.

"I remember that from kindergarten," Harlan said.

"This is a good book," Reggie added.

Stephanie didn't mind that the children were familiar with the book. Any good book is worth reading many times, and she planned to extend the story into a math activity.

After reading the book, Stephanie asked the children if they could describe something in the book that changed gradually. She noticed a couple of quizzical looks, so she asked, "Who knows what I mean by 'gradual'?"

Mark responded, "Does it mean a little at a time?"

"Yes," Stephanie answered. "When something changes gradually, it changes slowly over time, rather than suddenly or all at once."

Colleen raised her hand. "At the beginning of the book, everything is dark, and at the end, it's light."

"Did that happen a little at a time or all at once?" Stephanie asked. The class checked the illustrations to confirm that it was a gradual change.

Lamar answered next. "The bed went downer and downer when everybody was on it." The class returned to the book to look at the sagging mattress.

Next Maureen noticed that the rain stopped gradually as the sleepers woke up. Then Mary pointed out that characters began leaving the bed after the wakeful flea arrived.

Stephanie then posed a question. "When all the sleepers were piled up, how many feet were in the bed?" she suggested that they make a list of the characters in the story as a way to answer this question. As the class recalled the characters, Stephanie recorded them on the board, along with the number of feet each one had.

| | |
|---|---|
| *a snoring granny* | 2 |
| *a dreaming child* | 2 |
| *a dozing dog* | 4 |
| *a snoozing cat* | 4 |
| *a slumbering mouse* | 4 |
| *a wakeful flea* | 6 |

When the list was complete, some children immediately began counting on their fingers, while others seemed not to know how to figure out how many feet there were altogether. Stephanie offered a suggestion. "When I have to add a list of numbers like this, I look for pairs or groups of numbers that add up to ten. I'll show you." She drew a bracket connecting the 6 with the 4 above it and wrote *10* on the side. She explained what she was doing as she added the two remaining 4s together to make 8 and added a 2 to the 8 to get another 10. Now she had two 10s, and she added the last 2.

| | | | |
|---|---|---|---|
| *a snoring granny* | 2 | —— | 2 |
| *a dreaming child* | 2 | | |
| *a dozing dog* | 4 | > | 10 |
| *a snoozing cat* | 4 | | |
| *a slumbering mouse* | 4 | > | |
| *a wakeful flea* | 6 | | 10 |

Mark shouted, "Twenty-two!"

Next Stephanie introduced an individual assignment. "Now you're each going to make a house and think about the number of feet in it." Stephanie gave each child a piece of white $8\frac{1}{2}$-by-11-inch paper and demonstrated the origami folds needed to make a paper house, giving instructions as she folded. She took the students through the folds one step at a time. At each step, she asked a question to help them check their work: "Does your paper look like mine?"

Here are the directions for making the paper house:

1. Fold the paper in half, bringing the two $8\frac{1}{2}$-inch edges together. Then fold it in half again the other way.

2. Open the last fold. Hold the paper with the folded edge up. Then fold the outer sides into the middle fold.

3. Open the last two folds. Then put your finger inside one fold to separate the two parts and fold the inner part into the middle fold, making a triangle appear at the top.

4. Crease the paper so the two parts are open and there is a triangle at the top.

5. Do the same with the fold on the other side. The house should look like this:

Stephanie heard exclamations of delight as the children made the final folds to create the triangles for the roof.

"It really looks like a house!" Kimberly said.

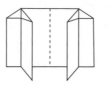

Stephanie held up her origami house and showed the children how to open the middle folds to see the inside of the house. She took a marker and began to sketch as she talked. "I'm going to show you who lives in my house," she said. She drew stick figures inside her paper house to represent herself, her husband, her son, her daughter, and their cat.

"Now let's count to find out how many feet live in my house," Stephanie said. Together, they counted twelve feet. She closed the doors of the house again and wrote *12* on the outside of one of the doors.

"Since we have twelve feet living in our house, my feet number is twelve," Stephanie said. "The feet number you'll write on your house will tell how many feet live inside."

Stephanie showed the children her house again and said, "Did you notice that I didn't spend a lot of time drawing my pictures? This kind of drawing is called sketching. A sketch is a quickly drawn picture that doesn't have a lot of details. I'd like you to make a sketch of the people who live in your house."

Mary raised her hand. "Can I draw my dog, Boris?" she asked.

"Sure," Stephanie said. "You should draw all living things that live in your house and have feet."

"Can I draw my fish?" Tom asked with a smile.

"Not unless your fish have feet," Stephanie replied.

The children began drawing, and a hush fell over the room. They were intent on their work. Even Ken, who had been wiggling and squirming through the whole lesson, was still and focused as he sketched. The connection to their own lives made this problem come alive for the children.

Stephanie walked around and observed the children working. She noticed that Timothy had written a *4* on the outside of his house.

She knew that there were four people in Timothy's family, so she asked him about it.

"What does this number mean?" she asked, pointing to the 4.

"Four people in my family," he replied.

"But how many feet live in your house? Your house number needs to tell that." Timothy still looked puzzled.

"Four would be the number of feet for just you and your brother, Justin," Stephanie said. "What about your mom's and dad's feet? You need to write the total number of feet in your house." Timothy erased the 4 and opened his house to count the feet again.

When the children had finished, Stephanie called for their attention. "Raise your hand if you think you have the smallest number of feet in your house," she said to begin a class discussion.

Cassie raised her hand. "Mine has ten feet," she said.

"Does anyone have a number of feet smaller than ten?" Stephanie asked.

Amy answered, "I have twelve."

"Is twelve smaller than ten or larger than ten?" Stephanie asked.

"Bigger," Amy answered.

"We're looking for a number that is smaller than ten," Stephanie reminded her.

Kimberly reported that she had six feet living in her house. "Does anyone have a number of feet that is smaller than six?" Stephanie asked. No one did, and the children agreed that six was the smallest number of feet living in any of their houses. Stephanie asked Kimberly to bring her house to the front of the room. Stephanie wrote the number 6 on the board and posted the house next to it. Then she asked other students with six feet in their houses to bring their houses to the front to post. She posted two more houses next to Kimberly's.

Then Stephanie asked, "Whose house might have the next smallest number of feet?" Nina told Stephanie her house had ten feet inside.

"Does anyone have a house with more than six feet and fewer than ten?" Stephanie asked. Heads went down around the room as children looked at their numbers.

Alexandra said, "I have eight," and brought up her house. Brenda, Timothy, Eddie, and Carol also brought their houses up for Stephanie to post. Each had an 8 written on the outside.

"Does anyone have a number between six and eight?" Stephanie asked.

Maureen raised her hand. "You can't, because seven is an odd number," she said.

"Can you explain what you mean, Maureen?" Stephanie asked.

"Legs are only even numbers," Maureen replied.

Mark shouted his agreement, "Legs come in twos and fours. You'd have to have a person with three legs to get seven!"

Stephanie wrote an *8* on the board under the *6* and posted the five houses. "How many more houses do we have with eight feet than with six feet?" Stephanie asked. The question of how many more is difficult for many first graders. Whenever a situation comes up where comparing numbers makes sense, Stephanie tries to ask this question. Children need to hear mathematical language spoken many times in order to learn to use it themselves. Also, they need to hear mathematical language used in contexts that allow them to make sense of the words.

When Lamar answered that there were two more houses with eight feet than with six feet, Stephanie asked him to explain how he figured that out. He came to the board and pointed to the two rows of houses. "These have matches on the six row," he said, pointing to the first three houses next to the number 8. "These two don't have matches, so that's two more."

Stephanie continued to call children up to post their houses. They had rows marked 6, 8, 10, 12, 14, 16, 18, 20, and 24. Stephanie pointed to one of the houses in the row marked 10.

"What could live in this house?" she asked.

"I don't know—that's not mine," Brenda said.

"Without peeking inside the doors, though, can you think of what might live in here?" Stephanie asked.

Cindy answered. As she spoke, Stephanie recorded what she said on another section of the board. "A mom, a dad, a sister, a brother," Cindy said and then stopped. On the board, Stephanie recorded a list: *Mom—2, Dad—2, Sister—2, Brother—2.* Cindy looked at the board, her lips moving as she counted silently. Then she added, "And a baby." Stephanie added *Baby—2* to the list and had the children count together by twos to verify that the number of feet was ten.

"Who can tell me another group of living things that could be in that house?" Stephanie asked. She called on Timothy.

"A dog," he said. Stephanie wrote: *Dog—4.* "A mom, a dad, and a cat," he added. Stephanie listed what he said, along with the number of feet for each.

"Let's add these to check," Stephanie said.

She pointed to the two 4s and the class said, "Eight."

As Stephanie pointed to the first 2, Eddie said, "Uh-oh. That's ten and we haven't counted the dad."

"Well, we could get rid of the dad," Stephanie said, and she erased that line.

Several children protested. "No, no." "Don't get rid of the dad." Apparently, Stephanie had hit a nerve. She wrote *Dad* again but accidentally put a 4 next to it instead of a 2.

"Hey, dads don't have four feet!" Mary exclaimed. Stephanie replaced the 4 with a 2. Finally the children decided to replace the cat with a sister.

Stephanie asked for other suggestions for the house with ten feet. Penny offered this group: Mom—2, Dad—2, cat—4, and bird—2. Coleen suggested Grandma—2, parrot—2, hamster—4, and Grandpa—2. Stephanie listed both of their suggestions on the board.

With four different groups of living things on the board, she asked, "Do you think these are all the ways that there could be ten feet in this house?" Most of the class felt sure that there were more possible solutions.

"I agree that there are more solutions to this problem," Stephanie said. "But instead of continuing to work on this problem, you're going to solve one of your own. Each of you will choose one house number to investigate. You'll try to find all the different groups of living things that could live in a house with that number of feet."

Stephanie then held up a sheet of 12-by-18-inch construction paper to demonstrate how they were to organize their work. "You need to fold a sheet of paper and write each new group you think of in a separate box." She demonstrated folding the paper in half, in half again the other way, and then in half once more.

"Stop before you open the paper," Stephanie said. "How many boxes do you think there will be when the paper is open?"

Children began shouting out numbers, so she asked for quiet. She heard the numbers four, five, six, and eight.

"Whisper to the person next to you what you think," Stephanie said. Whenever she has the opportunity, Stephanie wants children to think about numbers and their connections to little things the children do every day. She heard a sound of wonderment as they opened the paper and counted eight boxes.

The children worked intently. Some drew pictures of families, while others made lists like the ones on the board. Stephanie noticed that some students changed the number of living things in the house as they moved from box to box on their paper. She asked for the students' attention and clarified the directions about choosing one number to explore. "Stick with one feet number for the whole page," she said. "If you choose the number twelve, you need to find as many different solutions for twelve as you can." (See Figure 6–1.)

Figure 6–1: Sandi wrote lists and drew pictures of people, animals, and insects.

The room was quiet as the children wrote and drew. Audrey raised her hand, and Stephanie went to her desk.

"I'm stuck," Audrey told Stephanie.

"What's your feet number?" Stephanie asked. Audrey pointed to the 6 on her paper.

"What can live in this house?" Stephanie asked.

"A bird," Audrey replied.

"Write that in one box on your paper," Stephanie directed. Audrey wrote *bird* and also wrote a *2* next to it. This let Stephanie know that Audrey basically understood the problem but just needed some reassurance that she was on the right track.

She continued asking Audrey what else lived in the house and had her record her answers. After Audrey completed one box, Stephanie left her to work on her own.

Stephanie noticed Eddie's hand up and walked over to him. "I have nineteen feet already, and I can't think of anything alive that has only one foot," he said.

"Well, Eddie," Stephanie said, "I can't think of anything with only one foot either. What else might be the problem?"

"Maybe I counted wrong," Eddie said with a sigh. "I'll try again." When Stephanie looked in Eddie's direction a little while later, he smiled and gave her a thumbs-up sign. He had found and fixed his counting error.

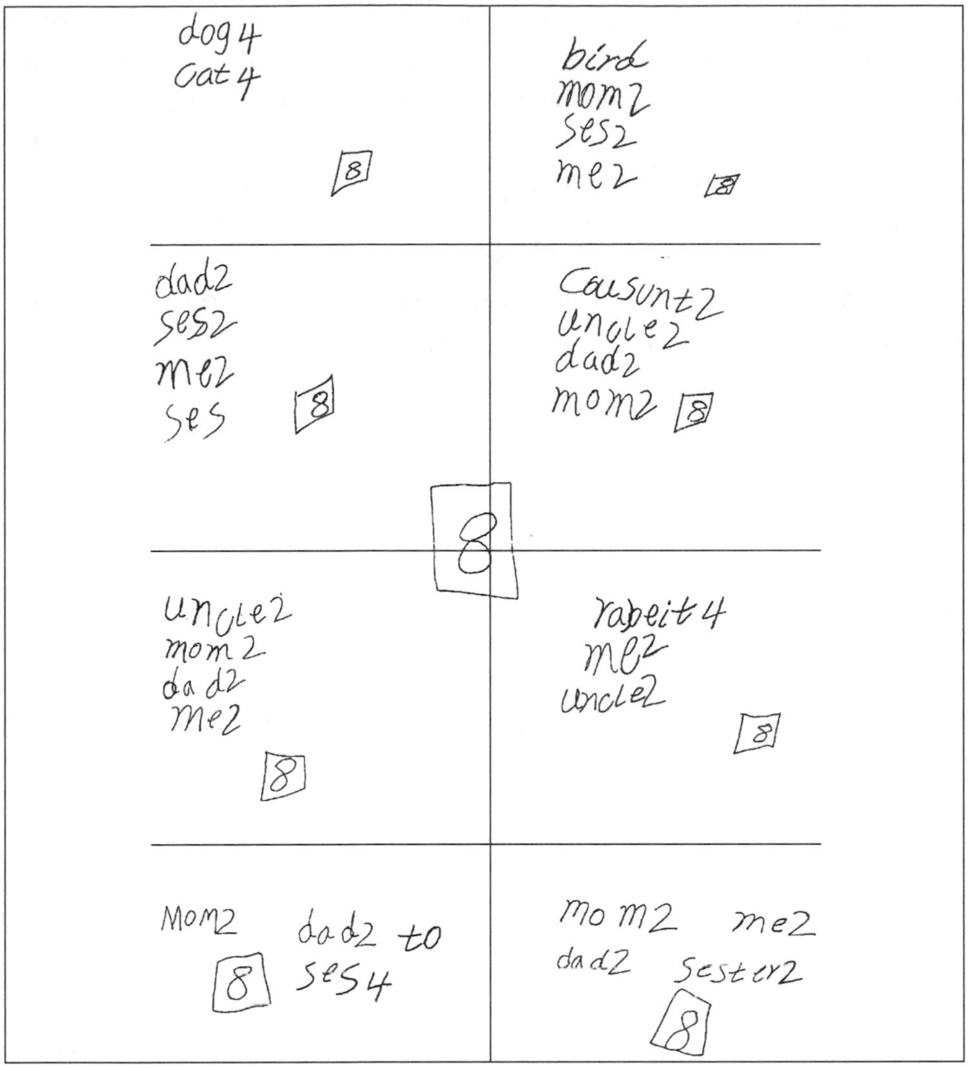
dog 4
cat 4
8
bird
mom 2
ses 2
me 2
8
dad 2
ses 2
me 2
ses
8
Causunt 2
uncle 2
dad 2
mom 2
8
8
uncle 2
mom 2
dad 2
me 2
8
rabeit 4
me 2
uncle 2
8
Mom 2
dad 2 to
ses 4
8
mom 2
me 2
dad 2
sester 2
8

Figure 6–2: Alexandra found eight ways to show eight feet in a house.

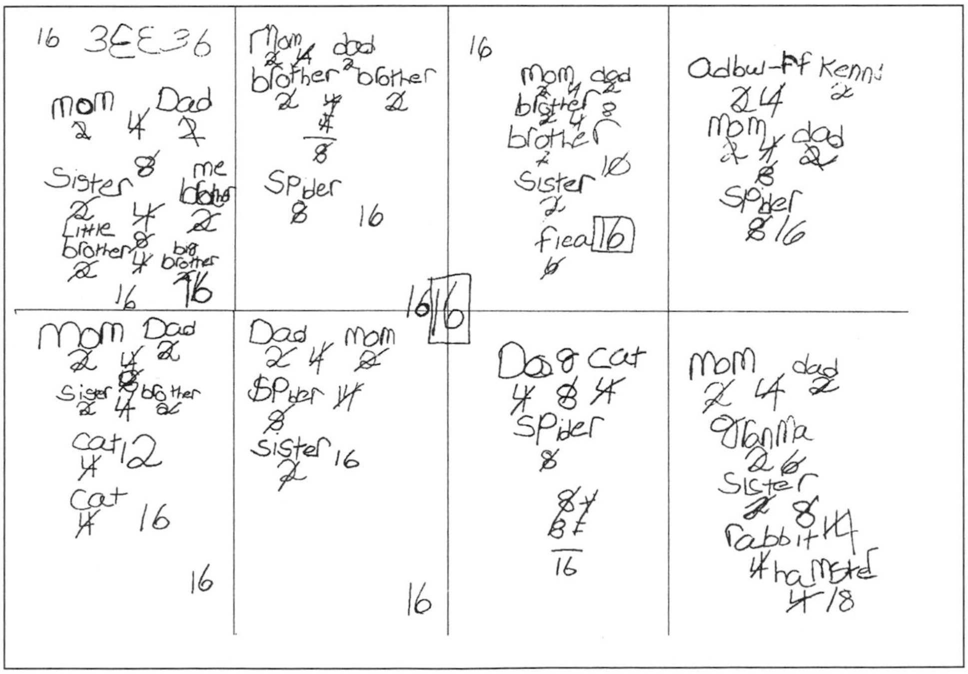
16
mom
Dad
Sister
16
Spider
8
16
16
Sister
flea
16
Spider
8/16
16
Mom
Dad
cat
16
16
Dad
mom
sister
16
16
Spider
16
mom
dad
Sister
rabbit
4/18

Figure 6–3: Ahmed discovered an efficient way to find sixteen feet. In many of his examples, he included a spider (eight feet) or a flea (six feet).

One of Stephanie's goals for students in first grade is to help them develop a sense of self-sufficiency about their problem solving. She wants them to understand that they are competent mathematicians in their own right and can verify their own answers. This problem encourages that kind of confidence. The numbers are manageable, the problem can have a number of solutions, and children can check their own answers in a variety of ways. Stephanie also likes that children have to decide for themselves when they are finished. (See Figures 6–2 and 6–3 on page 43 for two more students' papers.)

# One Monday Morning

*Taught by Stephanie Sheffield*

Uri Shulevitz wrote and illustrated *One Monday Morning* (2003). One Monday morning, a king, a queen, and a prince try to pay a visit to a little boy. The boy is not home, so the king, queen, and prince return with a knight on Tuesday. On Wednesday, the king, queen, prince, knight, and a royal guard try to visit the boy. The group of visitors keeps returning and growing until the boy is finally home to greet them. The story leads nicely to creating a concrete graph. Stephanie Sheffield reads the book to a first-grade class in this lesson and engages children in thinking about a counting problem.

## MATERIALS

interlocking cubes of various colors, 100 per
  pair of students

Stephanie used the big-book version of *One Monday Morning* to present the story to the first graders. As she read, children predicted the days. "Thursday's next," Kimberly said after Stephanie read what had happened to the boy on Wednesday. Students also predicted who was coming to visit the next day.

Stephanie read the book with the class several times over the next few days. Then she asked the students to help her recall the story without looking at the book. Their responses assured Stephanie they were familiar with the story, and she introduced the math activity.

"Today, we'll keep track of the number of visitors the boy had each day," Stephanie said.

She took out a bucket of Snap Cubes and had the children choose a color to represent each of Monday's visitors. Nina suggested yellow for the king, because it looked like gold and he wore a crown. The class chose red for the queen and blue for the little prince.

Harlan snapped one of each color together and stood the train of three cubes on the chalk tray. Stephanie wrote *Monday* above it, and then wrote the rest of the days of the week across the board, so they could put a train of cubes under each one.

Mary told the next part of the story. "They came back again on Tuesday," she said, "and the knight came, too."

Stephanie asked, "What color cubes should we use for Tuesday?"

Chris said, "Yellow, red, and blue, because all of them came back, and one more."

"Who else can explain Chris's idea?" Stephanie asked. She called on Russell.

"We need the same colors because the king, the queen, and the little prince came back on Tuesday," he said. "But we need a new color for the knight."

Mary suggested green, and Russell made a new stack with yellow, red, blue, and green cubes and stood it up on the chalk tray under Tuesday.

They continued in this way until they had retold the story through Thursday, building a train of cubes for each day. Stephanie then stopped to check that the children were relating the cubes to the story. She picked up the stack under Wednesday and pointed to the orange cube.

"Who can tell me what this orange cube stands for?" Stephanie asked. She wanted to reinforce for the children that the cubes represented the characters in the story. Stephanie knows that sometimes students lose touch with what manipulative materials represent when she doesn't give them opportunities to keep making connections between the materials and the situations. Several hands went up right away. She waited a few moments to give more children a chance to think and then called on Ronnie.

"Orange means the royal guard," she said.

"How do you know?" Stephanie asked.

"Because it's at the top, and the royal guard came last that day," Ronnie responded.

Then Stephanie asked, "I wonder, how could we figure out how many visitors came on Sunday?" Everyone talked at once. "Count the pictures in the book." "Make more stacks of cubes." "We could act it out." A few children began counting on their fingers.

"I'm hearing some wonderful ideas," Stephanie said. "I'm going to give you each the chance to think about the problem, figure it out, and explain what you did." The children were eager to get started, but Stephanie quieted them and told them she wanted to talk a bit more so they would be sure to understand what they were to do.

"What do we have in our classroom that you could use to help you figure out the number of visitors that came on Sunday?" Stephanie asked. Students responded by suggesting just about everything they had on the shelves—cubes, beans, tiles, links, and so on.

"You can use anything you think will help," Stephanie told them, "but I want you to think about how you are going to use the materials before you take them off the shelves. Also, I'm going to give each of you a sheet of blank paper so that you can record your answer and tell how you solved the problem." To suggest how they might begin writing, Stephanie wrote on the board: *On Sunday* _____ *visitors came.*

"You may use words, pictures, or numbers to help me understand how you solved the problem," Stephanie concluded.

The students began working in different ways. Some referred to the big book or to one of the small versions Stephanie had in the classroom. Some began writing right away. Others headed for the materials shelf. Some seemed at a loss for how to get started. Stephanie walked around, not intervening yet, but watching to see how each child approached the problem.

Mary drew pictures of seven people and a dog. When Stephanie asked Mary to tell her about her pictures, Mary identified each character in the story and then wrote letters above their heads so that Stephanie could tell who each was. "Every day another person came," Mary said.

"Can you write a number that will answer the question about how many visitors came on Sunday?" Stephanie asked. She left as Mary tried to think of another way to record her thinking.

Nina had more difficulty getting started. As Stephanie walked by, she wrinkled her forehead and said, "I don't know what to do." Nina often had trouble getting started on solving problems and looked to Stephanie for reassurance that she was on the right track.

"What do you think you might do first?" Stephanie asked.

"Copy the sentence off the board," Nina said tentatively. She did this and then carefully wrote the numbers from *1* to *12*. Stephanie told her she'd be back to check on her in a little while.

Russell used Snap Cubes to re-create what the class had built on the chalk tray. He made stacks of cubes beginning with a stack of three and continuing in a stairstep up to a stack of nine. He was smiling and eager to tell Stephanie about his solution. After he explained what he did, Stephanie asked him to think about what he could write on his paper that would show how he had solved the problem. "I know what to do!" he said. He drew pictures of the stacks of cubes and wrote a number on each one. (See Figure 7–1.)

Kimberly used the same strategy as Russell but explained that she also used the book to help her solve the problem.

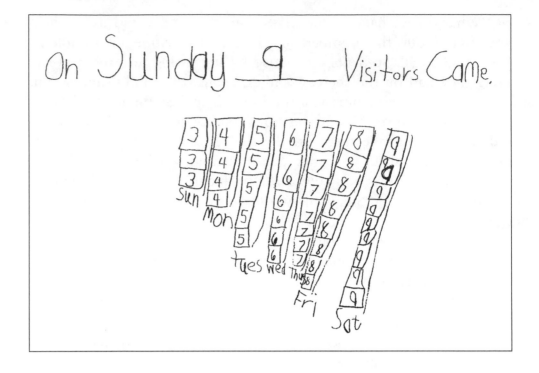

On Sunday __9__ Visitors Came.

Cal was finished before Stephanie got to his desk. He wrote: *i fegrit it at by 9.*

"How did you find that answer?" Stephanie asked.

"I looked at those cubes," he said, pointing to the stacks of cubes the class had built and placed on the chalk tray. While it was easy for Cal to look at those cubes and think ahead several steps to figure out how many there would be on Sunday, it was very difficult for him to put his process into words. Stephanie wasn't too worried about his difficulty, however. She knew that with many experiences of this kind, Cal would get better at explaining his thinking. With most things, practice is necessary for growth.

When Stephanie returned to Nina, she asked her how she had solved the problem. Nina smiled and said, "I figured it out with numbers."

"What do you think the answer is?" Stephanie asked.

Nina said, "I think it's a lot of numbers." Stephanie tried to interest her in trying to find just one number that would tell how many visitors came on Sunday, but Nina was perfectly happy with her answer. Stephanie wonders sometimes how much she should teach a child in a situation like this. She wasn't sure if Nina just didn't have a way to think about this problem or whether she really thought she had solved it and was happy with her answer. Stephanie decided to leave her singing a days-of-the-week song.

The children's work varied. Like Mary, Sharon drew pictures to solve the problem and labeled each picture with an initial to identify it. However, she left out the dog. (See Figure 7–2.)

Craig started to draw pictures of the cubes but erased them and instead drew pictures of the story characters. Maria drew pictures of cubes and characters and also copied the days of the week at the bottom, but she didn't seem able to come up with a final answer. (See Figure 7–3.)

The children's responses gave Stephanie hints about how individual students thought about the problem and what problem-solving strategies made sense to them.

Figure 7–3: Maria started to figure with Snap Cubes then seemed to get lost before finding a solution.

# Pattern Fish

*Taught by Leyani von Rotz*

In her book *Pattern Fish*, Trudy Harris (2000) weaves repeating patterns into humorous rhymes about sea creatures. The pattern for the wiggly, jiggly jellyfish, for example, is wiggle-jiggle-jiggle-float, wiggle-jiggle-jiggle-float. The same pattern is repeated visually in several other ways on the spread—in the pattern of squares at the top and bottom of the pages, in the birds flying across the top, and in other shape and color patterns. Finally, the text ends, leaving off the last word in the rhyme and thus inviting the children to use the patterns to predict the missing word, which is on the next page. At the end of the book, a section about patterns explains and illustrates patterns such as AB, AAB, and ABB. For this lesson, after reading the book to a kindergarten class, Leyani von Rotz reads it again and engages the children in searching for all of the patterns presented.

## MATERIALS

12-by-18-inch white construction paper, 2 sheets, each cut into 4 3-by-18-inch strips

## Day 1

"What do you see on the cover?" Leyani asked the kindergartners gathered around her. She held up her copy of *Pattern Fish* for them to study.

"Letters and fish," Gamila said.

"I see a snake S," Queenie said, noticing that the *s* in *fish* was also a snake.

Most of the children had raised their hands, eager to share what they saw. So that they all would have the chance to voice their ideas,

Leyani said to the children, "Turn and tell your partner what you see."

After a few moments, Leyani called the children back to attention to read the book aloud to them. "The name of this book is *Pattern Fish*," Leyani began. She opened the book to the first spread.

"Oooh, the fish is blowing bubbles," Kaisha said.

"There's a snail, too," Raul said.

Leyani read, "Yellow-black. Yellow-black. A fish swims in the ocean. It has stripes upon its back. Yellow-black, yellow-black, yellow . . . ." Leyani turned the page and read, "Black."

Leyani turned the page again to reveal a stripe-dot-dot pattern and read the rhyme to the children. "What do you think is on the next page?" Leyani asked.

"Dot!" a few children called out. Others hadn't yet caught on to the repeating pattern.

"You're right," Leyani responded. She turned the page and read, "Dot."

The book continues in this way, introducing different sea creatures and different patterns throughout—chomp-chomp-munch-munch, chomp-chomp-munch-munch; bubble-bubble-pop, bubble-bubble-pop; stretch-spurt-glide, stretch-spurt-glide; and so on. As Leyani continued reading, more of the children caught on to the idea that the repeating pattern was the clue to the word that came when she turned the page. By the end of the book, all were correctly predicting the missing word.

After finishing the book, Leyani read it again, this time stopping to talk about the different repeating patterns shown. She showed the children the first spread again, with the yellow-and-black-striped fish. Pointing to the stripes on the fish, Leyani said, "Let's say the pattern together—yellow, black, yellow, black, yellow . . . ."

Although Leyani stopped there, most of the children said, "Black."

"How did you know that the next color was black?" Leyani asked the children.

"Because I see the black on the fish," Danny said.

"Because it comes after yellow," Fawziya said.

"Yes, the stripes are in a yellow-black, yellow-black pattern, and the pattern repeats over and over again," Leyani said. "Do you see any other patterns on the page? What about the colors of the squares going across the top?"

The children began to chant the colors, "Pink, yellow, pink, yellow, pink, yellow."

Leyani interrupted them. "So the colors of the squares go in a pattern. Do you see any other patterns on the page?"

"I see red, pink, red, pink," Queenie said, pointing to the stripes in the tails pictured in the lower right corner.

"Let's all say that pattern together," Leyani said. As she pointed to the stripes in one of the tails, the children said the pattern in unison.

"There's a pattern on the snail, too," Eduardo said. "It's purple, dot, purple, dot, like that." Again, Leyani had the children say the pattern as she pointed to the alternating purple rectangles and pink circles on the snail's back.

Before leaving the page, Leyani read the text again. This time practically all of the children correctly predicted that the word *black* would be on the next page.

All of the patterns on the first spread are AB patterns, with only two colors or words that repeat. The next spread, with the eel, shows all ABB patterns—stripe-dot-dot, stripe-dot-dot; yellow-red-red, yellow-red-red; big-little-little, big-little-little; black-yellow-yellow, black-yellow-yellow; and so on. As she did with the first spread, Leyani asked the children to look for patterns. When a child identified one, she asked all of the students to chant the pattern together.

The next spread introduces a sea horse. Leyani held up the book so all of the children could see it and asked the children to talk with their partners about the patterns they saw. The patterns on this spread are all AABB patterns. After the children had a chance to talk in pairs, as she had done with the other pages, Leyani led a discussion about the patterns the children saw.

The book continues with other patterns—AAB, ABC, ABBC, and ABCD. (Leyani didn't use the descriptions of AB, AAB, or any others like this, but instead used language that related to the illustrations in the book.) The children stayed interested in the book for the entire second reading.

Leyani then gave the children a chance to comment on the book. "What did you like about it?" she asked them.

"I like the jellyfish," Mansur said.

"The octopus was happy swimming," Bayard said. Leyani showed the children the spread of a grinning, gliding octopus.

"I like the sea horse," Eduardo shared.

"I like the shark 'cause the shark wanted a friend," Kaisha said.

"I like the crab," Deandra said.

"I like the whole story," Hallie said.

## Day 2

Before class the next day, Leyani reproduced six of the color patterns shown with squares at the top and bottom of the pages in the book. To do this, she cut two pieces of 12-by-18-inch white construction paper into 3-by-18-inch strips and drew a row of twelve squares on each, each about an inch and a half on a side. Then she colored the first eight squares on each strip as listed below; each pattern matched one of the border patterns shown in the book.

pink, yellow, pink, yellow, pink, yellow, pink, yellow
red, red, yellow, red, red, yellow, red, red, yellow
pink, pink, green, green, pink, pink, green, green
yellow, yellow, green, yellow, yellow, green, yellow, yellow
red, green, yellow, red, green, yellow, red, green
red, pink, green, green, red, pink, green, green

Leyani posted the first pattern. "Let's read the colors together and see if we can figure out the pattern," Leyani said to the children. With the children's help, Leyani colored in the blank squares to continue the pattern to the end of the strip.

Next Leyani had the children interpret the same pattern with movement. "Let's clap for the pink squares and pat our shoulders for the yellow squares." The children followed along as Leyani did this, saying, "Clap, pat, clap, pat, clap, pat, . . . ."

Leyani suggested another pair of movements for the pattern. "This time let's do ears, chin, ears, chin," Leyani said, using her index fingers to first touch her ears, then her chin, then her ears, and then her chin again. As Leyani continued, the children mimicked her movements, some joining in and chanting, "Ears, chin, ears, chin . . . ."

Leyani continued in this way for the other patterns she had prepared, first having the children help her continue the pattern across the strip and then interpreting the pattern with movements. Leyani used children's suggestions for movements to use to interpret each of the patterns.

The book helped prepare the children for the pattern activities they would be experiencing over the next several weeks—building repeating patterns with interlocking cubes and pattern blocks, coloring in patterns on blank rows of squares, pasting a variety of shapes into patterns, playing follow the leader with clap-and-pat and other patterns, and chanting verbal patterns such as "ding-dong, ding-dong" and "oom-pa-pa, oom-pa-pa."

# A Pig Is Big

*Taught by Leyani von Rotz*

The opening spread of Douglas Florian's book *A Pig Is Big* (2000) asks, "What's big?" The book then takes the reader on a rhymed exploration of things that are big, bigger, and biggest, from a pig to a cow, to a truck, to a street, and eventually to the universe. Leyani von Rotz reads the book to a kindergarten class in this lesson and engages the children in making their own books about things that are bigger than a pig and things that are smaller than a pig.

### MATERIALS

**9-by-12-inch drawing paper,** 2 sheets per student

Leyani gathered the kindergarten children on the rug and showed them the cover of *A Pig Is Big*, which shows the face of a big, smiling, pink pig. "What do you think is going to happen in this book?" Leyani asked.

"I think he's going to eat a lot of food and get bigger," Mansur said.

Leyani began to read the book to the class. She showed the first spread and read, "What's big?" She then turned the page and read, "A pig is big. A pig is fat. A pig is bigger than my hat. What's bigger than a pig?"

Leyani turned the page to reveal a picture of a cow. After reading the rhyme about the cow, she read the question, "What's bigger than a cow?" Several children offered ideas and Leyani turned the page to reveal a car.

Leyani continued in this way and read the entire book aloud. The children were delighted to see the things that continued to get bigger and bigger—a car, a truck, a street, a neighborhood, a city, the whole wide earth, and, finally, the universe.

Leyani then revisited the book with the children. She again showed them the picture of the pig and asked, "What do you think is bigger than a pig?"

"A house," Queenie answered.

"Trucks," Acacia added.

"The whole world," Kaisha said.

"I think a house, too," Bayard said.

"A flying saucer," Danny added.

Leyani then showed the picture of the cow and asked, "What's bigger than a cow?"

"A dinosaur," Mallika answered.

"A big building," Daria said.

"How about a big truck?" Eduardo said.

Leyani turned the page to reveal the car and asked, "What's bigger than a car?" Many children were waving their hands, bursting with comments and eager to share their ideas. Leyani put the book down and said to the class, "Talk to your neighbor about what you think is bigger than a car."

After a few moments, to get the children's attention again, Leyani began a clapping pattern—clap, clap, pat, pat—and said, "When you see me, follow my pattern." In a few moments, all of the children had stopped talking and were clapping along with her. Leyani held the book up again and turned the page, revealing that a truck is bigger than a car. "What's bigger than a truck?" she asked.

"The movies," Gamil said.

"A big, big, big, big blue whale," Queenie said.

"Over there," Rico said, pointing to a picture of a blue whale posted on the far side of the room.

Leyani continued in this way for the rest of the book. When she reached the last page, she read again what was written about the universe: "It is the biggest thing of all. Compared to it all things seem small."

After a brief time for the children to report what they liked about the book, Leyani explained what they were going to do next. "In a moment, you'll each go to your table and draw two pictures. One should be of something that you think is bigger than a pig, and the other should be of something that you think is smaller than a pig. Think quietly in your head about what you might draw."

Leyani gave the children a few moments to think. She then said, "When you have an idea, raise your hand, and I'll give you one sheet of drawing paper to take to your table and draw something that's bigger than a pig. When you've finished that, I'll give you a piece of paper for you to draw something that's smaller than a pig." She dismissed the children one by one.

"There's a lot of big things in the book," Gamil commented as he took his piece of drawing paper.

After the children had finished their drawings, Leyani invited them back to the rug to share their work. After quieting the children, Leyani asked, "Raise a hand if you want to tell us what you drew that's bigger than a pig."

"I made a big circle," Eduardo said.

"I colored the sun," Fawziya reported.

"A swimming pool," Rico said.

"Me, too," Bayard added. "I like going to the swimming pool."

"I made the whole wide world," Gamil said.

"I made a building, a sun, and a man, and a box," Mansur stated, showing his complicated drawing.

As the children shared, Leyani jotted down what they said about their pictures. She then asked, "Who wants to tell us what you drew that's smaller than a pig?" Again, as children reported, Leyani recorded their descriptions.

"A baby," Danny reported.

"I made a flower," Deandra said.

"I made a mouse," Acacia said.

This ended the lesson for the day, and Leyani gathered the children's artwork to compile into two books—*What Is Bigger Than a Pig?* and *What Is Smaller Than a Pig?* She wrote each child's words on a separate sheet of paper and assembled the book so that each spread had the child's words on the left-hand side and his or her picture on the right-hand side.

## A Follow-up Activity

A few days later, Leyani gathered the children again, this time to read their class books to them. She held up What Is Bigger Than a Pig? and read the title to them. She went through each page in the book, inviting the children to read along with her if they could. Children offered comments about one another's artwork. For example, when Leyani showed Eduardo's drawing of a large circle, Kaisha said, "I like it. I like green and blue."

Mansur added, "It's pretty."

Rico and Bayard had both drawn swimming pools, and Gamil and Kaisha had both drawn buildings. Leyani showed the class Rico's and Bayard's drawings and asked the children to describe what was the same and what was different about them. She then asked them to compare Gamil's and Kaisha's drawings. For Mansur's drawing of a building, a sun, a man, and a box, Leyani asked, "Which of these things on Mansur's drawing is the biggest?" (See Figures 9–1 through 9–3 for three students' drawings.)

Leyani then followed the same procedure and read their other book, *What Is Smaller Than a Pig?* (See Figures 9–4 and 9–5 for two drawings from the book.) She then put the books in the class library for the children to enjoy on their own.

Figure 9–1: Queenie decided that "a big, big rectangle" was bigger than a pig.

Figure 9–2: To describe what he drew that was bigger than a pig Fawziya said, "I colored the sun."

Figure 9–3: For something that was bigger than a pig, Kaisha drew a building.

Figure 9–4: Deandra thought that a flower was smaller than a pig.

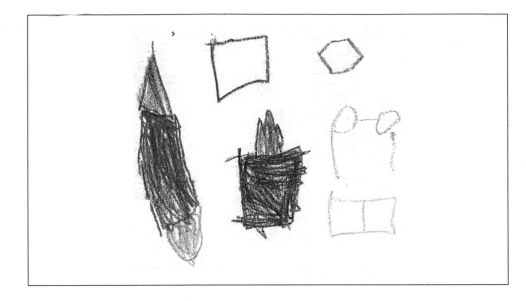

Figure 9–5: "I drew a pencil, a present, and play glasses, and some blocks," Mallika reported for her drawing of things that were smaller than a pig.

# Quack and Count

*Taught by Leyani von Rotz*

Each spread of Keith Baker's book *Quack and Count* (1999) shows seven ducklings in a different grouping. As the ducks move through the marsh and reeds, step onto the shore, splash into the water, and finally fly away, children see how the number seven can be broken apart into two addends in various ways. During this lesson, Leyani von Rotz reads the book to a class of first graders, and then connects the action in the story to number sentences for different ways to show the sum of seven. The children then choose and illustrate number sentences.

**MATERIALS**

Leyani read *Quack and Count* aloud to the first graders, reading the rhyme presented on each spread that introduces a combination of seven. For example:

*7 ducklings, 5 plus 2*
*Playing games of peekaboo*

The children counted first the ducks on the left-hand page, then the ducks on the right-hand page, and finally all seven together.

Leyani read the book again, this time stopping on each page to record a number sentence to go with the rhyme. For example, for the spread quoted above, Leyani said, "Watch as I write a number sentence for this page." On the board Leyani wrote $5 + 2$ and then asked, "And how much is five plus two?" It was obvious to some children that the answer was seven, but others had to count the objects on the page, and some used their fingers to figure.

Leyani showed the children the next page. "What number sentence should I write for this page?" she asked.

"Four plus three," Natalie said. Leyani recorded 4 + 3 and asked, "What do I have to write to finish the sentence?"

"You make an equals sign and then write seven," Anna said with confidence. As with the first sentence, some children had to count or figure to verify that 4 + 3 was equal to 7.

After continuing in this way for the next two spreads in the book, Leyani had recorded the following on the board:

$$6 + 1 = 7$$
$$5 + 2 = 7$$
$$4 + 3 = 7$$
$$3 + 4 = 7$$

Before continuing, Leyani asked the children, "What do you notice about the number sentences I wrote on the board?"

"They all make seven," Hassan said.

Clauda added, "Oh, look, the numbers in front are going down. It's six, then five, then four, then three, down like that."

"I see numbers going up," Travis said.

"Which numbers are you looking at?" Leyani asked Travis.

"Those ones in the middle," Travis answered. "See, they go one, two, three, four."

Vincent focused on the plus signs. "It goes plus, plus, plus, plus," he said.

"Oh yeah," Tyrone added, "and it goes equals, equals, equals, equals."

"Who has an idea about what number sentence I'll write next?" Leyani then asked. About half of the students raised their hands and Leyani called on Elana.

"I think it will be two plus five," she said matter-of-factly. Others nodded, but some children weren't so sure. Leyani returned to the book and turned the page to reveal the next spread, showing two ducks about to dive into the water and five ducks in the water already swimming.

"I was right," Elana said, pleased.

Leyani recorded 2 + 5 and asked, "How much is two plus five?" Again, some children needed to count or figure, while others either knew or were comfortable relying on the pattern of all sevens. After the next page, the list looked like this:

$$6 + 1 = 7$$
$$5 + 2 = 7$$

$$4 + 3 = 7$$
$$3 + 4 = 7$$
$$2 + 5 = 7$$
$$1 + 6 = 7$$

"If we follow the patterns we talked about, what number sentence would come next?" Leyani asked. "What would the first number be?"

"Zero," several children volunteered.

"Yes," Leyani said and read the first numbers, pointing to each as she moved her finger down the list. "Six, five, four, three, two, one, and then comes . . . ." She paused to give the children a chance to respond.

This time, more of them chorused, "Zero."

Leyani wrote a plus sign and asked, "What number comes next? Let's follow the pattern." As she did with the first numbers, she read down the list of the second addends, pointing to each.

"Seven," most of the children chimed in when Leyani reached the end.

"And seven goes at the end," Farrell said.

"Let's check," Leyani said, going down the list of sums, reading seven over and over again to reinforce the pattern.

"Who can read this last number sentence?" Leyani asked.

Ramya read, "Zero plus seven makes seven."

"What is this sign called?" Leyani asked, pointing to the equals sign. It's typical for children to read the equals sign as "makes," and Leyani wanted to reinforce its correct name. Equivalence is an important idea for young children to learn.

"Equals," several children answered.

"Yes," Leyani responded and then asked, "Is zero plus seven equal to seven? Do zero and seven add up to seven?" Most children agreed quickly that this was so; a few seemed unsure. Leyani showed the children the last illustration in the book of all seven ducks flying.

Leyani then asked, "If I wanted to add a sentence to the top of the list, what sentence could I write? Talk with your neighbor about your idea and raise a hand when you're ready to tell what you think." After a few moments, Leyani called the class to attention and had the children say the sentence together in a whisper voice. Leyani added it to the top of the list.

$$7 + 0 = 7$$
$$6 + 1 = 7$$
$$5 + 2 = 7$$
$$4 + 3 = 7$$

$$3 + 4 = 7$$
$$2 + 5 = 7$$
$$1 + 6 = 7$$
$$0 + 7 = 7$$

Leyani then wrote two of the number sentences to the side of the list, one underneath the other:

$$6 + 1 = 7$$
$$1 + 6 = 7$$

"Why do you think I wrote these two together like this?" Leyani asked.

Farrell responded, "They're the same numbers."

Leyani said, "So what's the same about them is that they use the same numbers, six, one, and seven." As she said each number, Leyani pointed to it in the first number sentence. Then she repeated the numbers, pointing to them in the second number sentence.

"What's different about the two number sentences?" Leyani then asked.

"They're switched around," Travis said.

"Which are switched around?" Leyani probed.

Travis said, "See, it's six and one, and then it's one and six." Leyani pointed to the numbers to illustrate Travis's idea.

"Are there other pairs of number sentences that switch the numbers we add?" Leyani asked. With the children's help, she recorded the other pairs of number sentences in the same way.

To introduce the idea that more than two addends can be combined, Leyani showed the class the page near the end of the book where all seven ducks have begun to fly. Even though the ducks are shown as one grouping, there are two ducks in front, followed by three ducks, with two ducks bringing up the rear. Leyani recorded the related number sentence:

$$2 + 3 + 2 = 7$$

"Who can tell me what this first two in my number sentence tells us?" Leyani said, first pointing to the 2 and then to the illustration in the book.

"It's those two ducks," Hallie said, pointing to the two ducks at the left flying together.

"And what does this three tell us?" Leyani continued. Vincent pointed to the three ducks in the middle of the illustration.

"And the next two?" Leyani continued. Hassan pointed to the pair of ducks in front.

"And what does the number seven tell us?" Leyani concluded.

Anna said, "It's all of them together."

Then Leyani showed the children the next page, the next-to-last page in the book, with all seven ducks flying "up and up into the sky." Leyani pointed out the two in the rear flying together, the next two flying together, two new the front, and the one duck leading the formation. She recorded:

$$2 + 2 + 2 + 1 = 7$$

As Leyani did for the numbers in the previous sentence, she asked children to relate each of the numbers in the sentence to the ducks in the illustration.

Finally, Leyani showed the children the last page, which shows the numeral 7 formed by the seven flying ducks. "I see three ducks here and four here," Leyani said, pointing to the three ducks that form the top of the numeral and the four ducks going down. She wrote $3 + 4$ on the board. "How many ducks are there altogether?"

"Seven," the children said in unison.

Leyani added $= 7$ to complete the number sentence, saying, "Three plus four equals seven."

Tyrone saw the ducks differently. "I see those five flying together," he said, moving his finger up and down to identify the five ducks stacked vertically, forming the downward stroke of the numeral. He concluded, "And then there are those two," pointing two fingers to the ducks at the top of the numeral.

"And which number sentence matches what Tyrone sees?" Leyani asked the class, pointing to all of the number sentences on the board. The children scanned the list. Some picked out $2 + 5 = 7$ and others identified $5 + 2 = 7$.

Leyani then gave the children an individual assignment. She said, "Pick one of the number sentences from the board and copy it onto your paper. Then draw something to show what the number sentence means. You can draw ducks, or shapes of any kind, or anything you'd like." The children were interested in the assignment and tackled it eagerly.

As an extension for those who worked more quickly, Leyani gave children who completed the assignment another sheet of paper folded into four sections. She explained, "Now you can do four other sentences, each in one of the spaces on this new paper." (See Figures 10–1 through 10–5.)

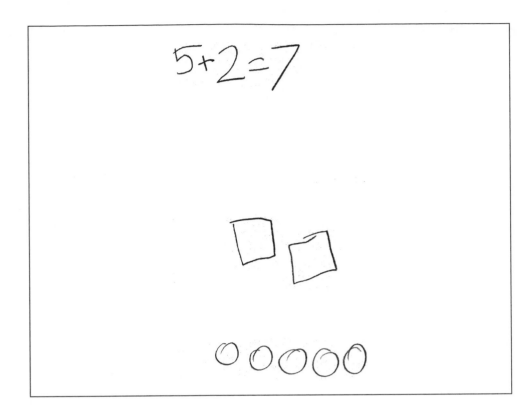

Figure 10–1: Ramya chose 5 + 2 = 7 and drew five circles and two squares.

Figure 10–2: Jerilyn illustrated two number sentences and included extra artwork as well.

Figure 10–3: Phillip drew
circles for the two addends
and for the total.

Figure 10–4: Clauda
illustrated 4 + 3 = 7.

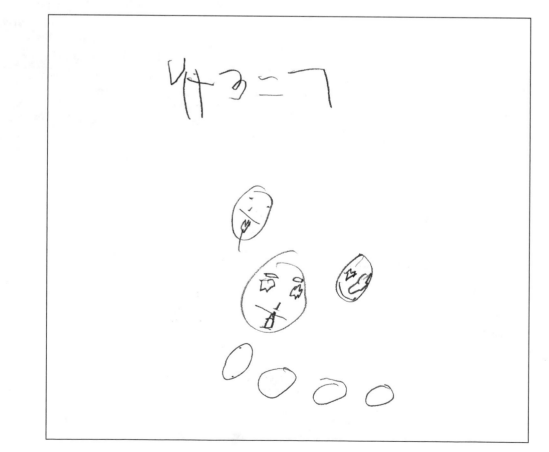

Figure 10–5: Natalie drew hearts for the extension assignment. While the groupings weren't obvious for all of the number sentences, Natalie was clear about how she formed the groups.

# Ready or Not, Here I Come!

*Taught by Leyani von Rotz*

Teddy Slater's book *Ready or Not, Here I Come!* (1999) draws on two real-world experiences—playing hide-and-seek, and a younger child wanting to play with the "big kids." Emma's little sister, Maggie, wants to play hide-and-seek with Emma and her two friends, Rose and Lulu. The older girls initially don't want to include Maggie but give in after Emma insists that Maggie can count to one hundred. Emma is It but counts slowly, leaving the other girls plenty of time to play several speedier games by counting to hundred by fives, tens, and twenties. In this lesson, Leyani von Rotz reads the book to a class of first graders and then engages the children with thinking about counting to hundred by ones, fives, tens, and twenties.

## MATERIALS

Leyani showed the first graders the cover of the book and said, "The title of this book is *Ready or Not, Here I Come!* What do you notice about the cover? And what do you think this book is about?"

Peter shared first. "The girl is counting. See, she's saying ninety-eight, ninety-nine, a hundred." Peter noticed the speech balloon with the numbers in it.

"They're playing hide-and-seek!" Elana said.

"You can see the others hiding," Hallie added.

"Raise a hand if you have ever played hide-and-seek," Leyani said. Most of the children raised their hands. Several wanted to tell about their hide-and-seek experiences, but Leyani moved the lesson forward by beginning to read the book aloud. The children enjoyed the story.

"I liked the part where the sister let her play and gave her a hug," Jamila offered.

"I liked how they hugged her at the end," Clauda said.

"I know how to count to one hundred," Tyrone said proudly.

"Me, too," several others chimed in.

Next, Leyani wrote *Maggie* on the board and asked, "Why didn't Emma and her friends want Maggie to play hide-and-seek with them?"

"They thought she was too little," Ramya said.

"Because she counted too slow," Travis added, rolling his eyes.

Leyani responded, "Well, Maggie did count slowly, but she was able to count all the way to one hundred without making a mistake." Leyani opened the book to the page where Maggie begins to count and directed the children's attention to the numbers 1, 2, 3 at the top of the page. Leyani read the numbers aloud and then turned the page to reveal the numbers 4, 5, 6 at the top. Leyani read these, and again turned the page and read the numbers. The children joined in and began to count along with Leyani, and they continued until they reached hundred.

"So Maggie counted by ones all the way to one hundred," Leyani said and recorded next to where she had written Maggie's name on the board:

*Maggie*         *1, 2, 3, 4, 5, 6, 7, 8, . . . , 100*

Leyani explained, "I didn't want to write all of the numbers, so I put the dots in to show that I know that I left out lots of them." She then continued, "Because Maggie was counting so slowly, the girls decided to play a quicker game on their own—speed hide-and-seek. Rose was It. Who remembers what Rose counted by to get to one hundred?"

The children had several answers. Leyani then turned to the page showing Rose counting by fives. "Why would counting by fives to one hundred be speedier than counting by ones?" Leyani asked. "Talk with the person next to you about why counting by fives is faster than counting by ones." It seemed obvious to the children that counting by fives was quicker, and when Leyani asked for their attention, several had explanations.

"You don't have to say all the numbers," Farrell shared.

"You just go five, ten, fifteen, twenty, like that, and it's quick," Paulo said.

Leyani again showed the children the page where Rose begins to count by fives. While the numbers that Maggie is saying appear at the top of the page, the numbers that Rose is saying are at the bottom of the page—5, 10, 15, 20, 25, 30, 35, 40. After reading these aloud together, Leyani turned the page and, with the children joining in, continued the pattern of counting by fives up to hundred.

Underneath what she had recorded for Maggie, Leyani wrote *Rose* and her counting sequence, saying the numbers as she did so.

| | |
|---|---|
| *Maggie* | *1, 2, 3, 4, 5, 6, 7, 8, . . . , 100* |
| *Rose* | *5, 10, 15, 20, 25, . . . , 100* |

Then Leyani said, "Rose didn't say all of the numbers the way Maggie did. She skip-counted by fives."

Leyani then pointed to the dots she had inserted between 25 and 100. "Who can tell me what the dots mean?" she asked.

"They're for the missing numbers," Vincent said.

Leyani showed the children the page in the book where Rose reaches hundred, with the numbers at the bottom of the page. The top of the same page shows that Maggie has only counted up to sixty. "So the girls decided to play super-speed hide-and-seek," Leyani said. "This time Lulu was It, and she skip-counted by tens. Let's count together to one hundred by tens." The children chanted the numbers along with Leyani. Leyani then had them read the numbers from the bottom of the pages that show Lulu counting. Leyani again recorded on the board.

| | |
|---|---|
| *Maggie* | *1, 2, 3, 4, 5, 6, 7, 8, . . . , 100* |
| *Rose* | *5, 10, 15, 20, 25, . . . , 100* |
| *Lulu* | *10, 20, 30, 40, 50, . . . , 100* |

Leyani again showed the children the page where Lulu reaches hundred. "How is Maggie doing with her counting?" she asked.

"She's only up to eighty-two," Jerilyn said, referring to the numbers at the top of the page.

"Then they played again," Anna said.

"Yes," Leyani responded. "Now Emma was It and she skip-counted by twenties in just one breath." Leyani showed the children the page with Emma counting in one breath.

"Let's try it. Let's take a deep breath and count by twenties to one hundred," Leyani said. Leyani and the children all took a breath and chanted in unison, "Twenty, forty, sixty, eighty, one hundred."

"She and Maggie got to one hundred at the exact same time," Clauda said with a giggle. Others giggled, too.

"But Maggie tagged them, so she won," Tyrone added.

Leyani nodded and recorded how Emma had counted.

| Maggie | 1, 2, 3, 4, 5, 6, 7, 8, . . . , 100 |
| Rose | 5, 10, 15, 20, 25, . . . , 100 |
| Lulu | 10, 20, 30, 40, 50, . . . , 100 |
| Emma | 20, 40, 60, 80, 100 |

"Hey," Travis said, "you didn't put those dots in."

"I didn't leave any numbers out this time," Leyani said. "I skip-counted by twenties and wrote all of the numbers—twenty, forty, sixty, eighty, one hundred. I only write dots when I don't write all of the numbers in the pattern." This seemed to satisfy Travis.

Leyani reviewed what was on the board, pointing to what she had written as she said, "So Maggie counted by ones, and Rose counted by fives." Leyani then stopped to record *Count by 1s* next to Maggie's numbers and *Count by 5s* next to Rose's numbers. She then reviewed how Lulu and Emma had counted and recorded for them, too.

| Maggie | 1, 2, 3, 4, 5, 6, 7, 8, . . . , 100 | Count by 1s |
| Rose | 5, 10, 15, 20, 25, . . . , 100 | Count by 5s |
| Lulu | 10, 20, 30, 40, 50, . . . , 100 | Count by 10s |
| Emma | 20, 40, 60, 80, 100 | Count by 20s |

Leyani said, "Counting by twenties is the fastest way to count to one hundred because we only have to say five numbers—twenty, forty, sixty, eighty, one hundred." Leyani pointed to the numbers as she said them.

Leyani continued, "Let's skip-count by tens and see how many numbers we have to say." The children counted by tens together, with Leyani putting up a finger for each number as they said it.

"So it takes ten numbers to count to one hundred by tens," Leyani said, holding all ten fingers up. She then asked, "How many numbers do you think it will take to count to one hundred if we skip-count by fives?" Some of the children guessed numbers and some shrugged. A few children began to count by fives to themselves, using their fingers to keep track. Some looked at the 1–100 chart posted in the room to figure out how many numbers it took. This question was out of reach for practically all of the children, and Leyani didn't push it. Instead, she said, "If we count to one hundred by ones, we have to say all of the numbers. That's one hundred numbers. That's why it took Maggie so long."

Leyani now gave the students an assignment. She said, "Think about which of these ways you would count to one hundred if you were playing hide-and-seek and you were It. Would you count the way Maggie did, or Rose, or Lulu, or Emma?" Leyani pointed to the board where she had recorded for each girl. She continued, "Then write down the numbers you would say to count to one hundred. But don't leave any numbers out or use dots the way I did on the board. You have to write all of the numbers until you get to one hundred, the way I did for Emma counting by twenties. Also, if you'd like, you can draw a hide-and-seek picture."

"We can count any way we want?" Clauda asked.

"As long as it's one of the ways from the story—by ones, fives, tens, or twenties," Leyani responded.

"This could be hard," Jamila commented.

"The easiest way to count is to do it Emma's way," Leyani suggested. "When I wrote the numbers for counting by twenties, I didn't leave out any of them, so they're all there to help you."

There were no other questions or comments, so Leyani asked the children to start their work.

"I'm going to draw me counting," Paulo announced as the children got busy.

As the children worked on the assignment, Leyani circulated and gave help as needed. Almost half of the students took Leyani's suggestion about counting by twenties, with some copying from the board and others figuring out the numbers for themselves.

David was one of only three children who decided to count by fives. He worked carefully and thoughtfully until he reached sixty-five. Then he stopped, wrote three dots, and brought his paper to Leyani. Leyani noticed that David had omitted thirty in his sequence and asked him to read the numbers aloud. "Point to each number as you say it," she said.

David discovered his own error. "Oops," he said and added *30* to his paper.

When he got to sixty-five, Leyani asked, "Can you continue the pattern all the way to one hundred?" David nodded and returned to his desk to do so.

Counting by tens was also a popular choice, and several children referred to the 1–100 chart posted in the room for help with the numbers. Several children counted by ones and seemed to enjoy writing all of the numbers. On his paper, Peter wrote the numbers in a large speech balloon over the picture of a child leaning against a tree and counting.

Leyani felt that the assignment not only gave her ways to talk to the children about the number sequences but also was, in general, a useful assessment. (See Figures 11–1 through 11–5 for several children's work.)

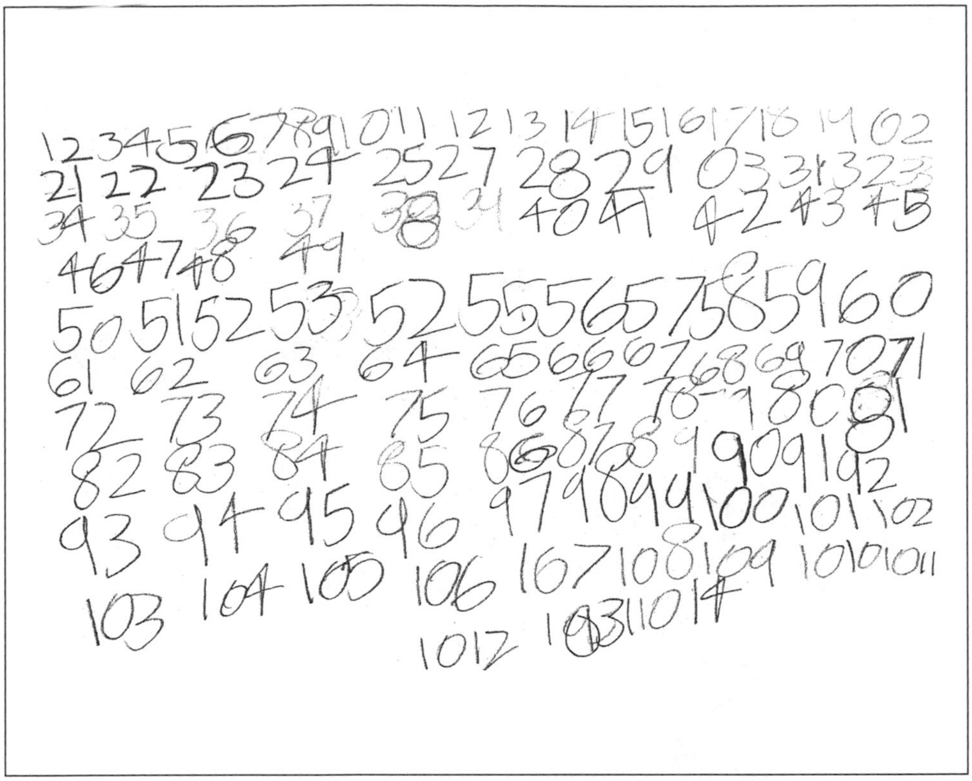

Figure 11–1: Jerilyn decided to count by ones and continued beyond 100 to 114. She incorrectly wrote the last five numbers as 1010, 1011, 1012, 1013, 1014, following the pattern for the numbers from 101 to 109. This is a common error for children this age.

Figure 11–2: Travis chose to count by tens.

Figure 11–3: Ramya counted by fives and wrote the entire sequence correctly.

Figure 11–4: David counted by fives, initially stopping when he reached sixty-five and writing three dots. Leyani asked him to complete the sequence and he did.

Figure 11–5: Jamila counted by twenties, quickly copying the numbers from the board and then spending the rest of the time on her drawing.

# Rooster's Off to See the World

*Taught by Olga Torres*

Eric Carle's book *Rooster's Off to See the World* (1972) is about a rooster who one fine day decides that he wants to travel. Soon other animals decide to join him. A problem arises, however, when night falls and they all realize that no plans have been made for food or shelter. Strikingly illustrated with colorful collages, the book provides a numerical problem-solving opportunity for young children. Olga Torres reads the book to a first-grade class in this lesson, and asks the children to figure out how many animals went off to see the world.

## MATERIALS

1 12-inch ruler

Olga gathered the first-grade children on the rug. When she showed them the cover of the book, Joey blurted out, "It's a rooster!"

"Yes," Olga said. "The title of this book is *Rooster's Off to See the World.*" Olga opened the book and held it so that the children could see how the illustration of the rooster continues on to the back cover.

"His tail is so beautiful," Carina commented.

"I like how the sun is smiling," Joy added.

"Let's find out what happens when the rooster goes off to see the world," Olga said. She opened the book to the beginning of the story.

"Look, it's the same picture as the cover," Eddie noticed.

"Yes, it is," Olga said. "Now listen quietly as I read the story to you." The first spread reveals that after setting off to see the world, the rooster begins to feel lonely. On the next spread, the rooster meets two cats and invites them to come along. They agree, and the three of them continue down the road. As they wander on, they meet three frogs. Eager for more company, the rooster invites the frogs to come along as well. They are then joined by four turtles, and then by five fish.

Once the sun goes down, however, and it begins to get dark, the animals begin to complain. "Where's our dinner?" "Where are we supposed to sleep?" They complain that they are cold. Then some fireflies fly overhead, and they complain that they are afraid.

Unfortunately, the rooster hasn't made any plans for the trip and doesn't know what to tell his friends. After a few moments of silence, the five fish announced that they are going home, and they swim away. Then the four turtles leave, followed by the three frogs, and then the two cats. Finally, the rooster returns to his own perch. After eating his meal of grain, he goes to sleep, dreaming about taking a trip around the world.

The children listened quietly and attentively to the story. Olga waited a moment after finishing the book to allow the children to enjoy the silence. Then she asked, "Who remembers the animals that joined the rooster on his trip?" Olga waited until almost all of the children had raised their hands. Then she called on Isabel.

"Isabel, tell us one of the animals that went off to see the world with the rooster," Olga said.

"Frogs," Isabel answered.

"Do you remember how many frogs joined the rooster?" Olga asked.

Isabel hesitated for a moment and then said, "Three."

"Yes, that's right," Olga said, opening the book to the spread that shows the frogs joining the rooster.

As Olga pointed to each frog, the children counted, "One, two, three."

Olga then pointed out the small illustrations in the upper right corner of the spread. One rooster is drawn in a square at the top, underneath are two squares with a cat in each, and underneath them are three squares with a frog in each. Olga said, "So first two cats joined the rooster, and then three frogs came along. What happened next?"

"The turtles came," Danny said. "There were four of them."

Olga turned the page and had the children count the four turtles as she pointed to them. They also noticed the row of four squares with a turtle in each that appear in the upper right corner of the page.

Olga said, "And next they were joined by five . . . ." Olga hesitated.

"Fish," the children said in unison, completing her sentence. Olga turned the page so the children could count the fish and look at the new row of five squares added to the corner showing the fish.

Olga then opened the book to show the children the pattern that appears on the inside front cover and the facing page. The same small illustrations used in the upper right corner of the pages appears in a repeating pattern of one rooster, one cat, one frog, one turtle, and one fish. As Olga pointed to the animals, the children named them.

Not only did the repeating pattern serve to help the children remember the animals for the problem they were going to solve, but it also gave Olga the opportunity to talk about the idea of repeating patterns. Using a ruler, she covered over part of one line in the pattern. A rooster was showing just in front of the edge of her ruler. "Do you know which animal comes next, that's under the ruler?" Olga asked.

Hands shot up and Olga asked the children to tell the animal in a whisper voice. "Cat," they whispered.

Olga slid the ruler to reveal the illustration of the cat. "How did you know that a cat came next?"

"It's the same on all of them," Lisa said.

"The cat always comes after the rooster," Travis added, pointing to several examples on the page.

"And next comes a frog," David said. Olga slid the ruler to reveal that David was correct.

Olga then said, "You can predict what comes next because you figured out the pattern. The pattern goes rooster, cat, frog, turtle, fish, rooster, cat, frog, turtle, fish." Olga pointed to the illustrations as she read the pattern and then read it once more so that the children could join in. "The pattern repeats over and over like this," Olga added. "This is an example of a repeating pattern."

Olga then opened the book to show the children the inside back cover. "Does this show the same pattern?" Olga asked. She gave the children a few moments to examine the illustrations before everyone agreed that the animals appeared in the same repeating pattern.

Olga then presented the problem for the students to solve. "Your job is to figure out how many animals altogether went off to see the world," Olga said. "Draw pictures, use numbers, and write about how you figure." As Olga gave the children paper, she dismissed them from the rug to return to their seats. She circulated, offering help to those who had difficulty getting started. When children completed their solutions, Olga asked them to explain their thinking.

Isaac used crayons to represent the animals and showed them with tallies on his paper. "I counted the crayons," he explained, "and they made fifteen. I put one crayon, two crayons, three, four, and five crayons. Then I counted them all together. I did this: one, two, three, four, five, six, seven, eight, nine, ten, and five makes fifteen."

Eddie drew boxes for the animals and numbered them. "I put them in boxes and counted them by one, two, three," he explained. (See Figure 12–1.)

"I did the initials of the animals," Beverly explained. "I counted with my pencil. I came up with fifteen."

Stephanie kept a running total as more animals joined the group. She recorded *1, 3, 6, 10,* and *15* on her paper and wrote: *15 animals went off into the world.* "I decided to add the animals," she explained. (See Figure 12–2.)

Rafael explained how he solved the problem. "I done one rooster," he said, "then two cats, three frogs, four turtles, and five fish. I colored them different colors. I counted them on my hands."

Not all the children were able to get the correct answer. Sharon, for example, described what she remembered of the story. She said,

Figure 12–1: After drawing boxes in a pattern to represent the animals, Eddie numbered them to find the total.

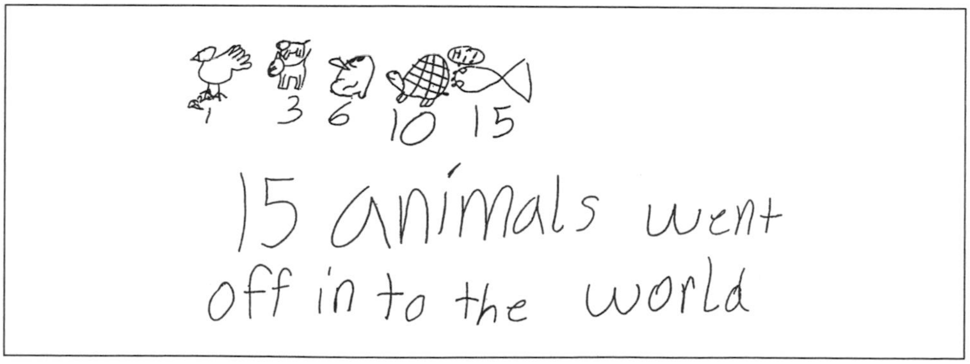

Figure 12–2: Stephanie kept a running total of the animals as they joined the group.

Figure 12–3: Danny was
one of the children who
didn't get the correct
answer.

12 animals

I counted all the animals when she was Reading the Story.

"Ten animals went around the world. The rooster was first, then two cats and then a frog and then a turtle and a fish."

Danny got the answer of twelve. He wrote: *I counted all the animals when she was reading the story.* (See Figure 12–3.)

Phillip didn't know how to find the total. "One rooster wanted to go around the world," he said, "and then he met two cats. Then he said, 'You want to go with me around the world?' Then three frogs went. Then went four fish and five turtles. I don't know the answer, but I wrote it down."

The students' papers and explanations revealed a variety of approaches and were useful for assessing the children's number understanding.

# The Shape of Things

*Taught by Leyani von Rotz*

Dayle Ann Dodds (1994) wrote that she developed the idea for *The Shape of Things* to help children see "how a few simple shapes make up a lot of things we have in the world." With engaging rhymes and bright illustrations, her book helps children see and, eventually, draw the world around them. In this lesson, after reading the book to a kindergarten class, Leyani von Rotz organizes three activities for the class to give the students further experience with identifying and naming shapes.

## MATERIALS

blocks in shapes similar to the shapes in the book—several sizes of squares, rectangles, triangles, and diamonds, at least 10 of each block

triangles, rectangles, circles, and squares cut from construction paper, each about the same size as the shapes shown on the left-hand pages in the book, at least 10 of each shape

Leyani gathered the kindergartners on the rug and showed them the cover of *The Shape of Things*. "What do you see on the cover?" she asked.

"I see a sun," Gamila said.

"A house," Acacia contributed.

"I see a boy and two girls," Tamera added.

"I see a house shape and a sun shape," Mansur said.

"There's a tree there and a tree there," Bayard said, pointing to the trees on each side of the house.

After all of the children who wanted to share had the chance to do so, Leyani opened the book and showed the class the first two-page spread. The left-hand page shows a large yellow square with a rhyme underneath it describing how squares can be found in a house's roof, windows, and door.

After reading the text, Leyani focused the children on the right-hand page. Pictured on this page is the yellow square transformed into a house, as shown on the book's cover. The house has two windows that are also squares, a red door, a roof, and two chimneys. The two trees that Bayard noticed on the cover are also in the picture.

"What do you notice on this page?" Leyani asked. Children reported several things that they noticed.

"A tree," Daria said.

"A window," Fawziya said.

"The roof," Acacia said.

Leyani then said, "So the yellow square was changed into a house. What else could you make with a square?" Several of the children suggested things that they saw in the illustration, such as a window and a roof. Daria suggested a school.

Before going on to the next page, Leyani pointed out the pattern in the top and bottom borders of alternating green and yellow squares, with the green squares larger. "Let's look at the pattern," Leyani said. Then, pointing to the squares across the top of the page, Leyani said, "Yellow square, green square, yellow square, green square, yellow square, . . . ." Soon all of the children joined in as Leyani followed the pattern across the two pages. Leyani did this again, this time focusing on the sizes of the squares, not the colors: "Little square, big square, little square, big square, little square, . . . ." Again, the children chimed in.

Leyani turned the page and showed the children the next spread. The left-hand page shows a blue circle, and the right-hand page shows a nighttime amusement park scene with the blue circle made into a ferris wheel. Before discussing the page with the class, Leyani asked the children to talk with their partners about the picture on the right-hand page. She told the children, "Talk about what you notice on the page, and then talk about what else you think you could make with a circle." The children became animated and the room became noisy. After a minute or so, Leyani asked the children for their attention. When they were all quiet, she asked, "Who would like to share what you talked about with your partner?"

Queenie said, "I talked about when I went on the roller coaster faster and faster."

"I saw the roller coaster and the kids," Gamila said.

"There's a mommy and a girl," Tamera added.

"And what else could you make with a circle?" Leyani asked.

"A clock," Danny said, pointing to the clock on the wall.

"A ball," Bayard added.

After the children had shared, and before turning to the next page, Leyani focused on the border pattern. This time the pattern showed alternating circles, a larger red circle and a smaller blue one. Again, Leyani described the pattern twice, once focusing on the circles' colors (red circle, blue circle, red circle, and so on) and then focusing on their sizes (big circle, small circle, big circle, and so on).

The next spread shows a red triangle on the left-hand page and, on the right-hand page, the red triangle turned into a boat with a green triangle for its sail. Leyani asked the same two questions: What do you notice? What else could you make with a triangle? She first gave the children the chance to talk with their partners and then led a discussion. Finally, they looked at the border pattern.

Leyani continued in this way for the remainder of the book. A rectangle was next, followed by an oval and a diamond. The last two spreads show many examples of things made from the shapes that have been introduced. Finally, the last spread is filled with rows of shapes, each row following a different pattern.

After reading the book, Leyani asked the children to look around the room for different shapes. "Find a rectangle in the room and point to it," she instructed. Then she asked the children to describe what they had found.

"A picture," Danny said, pointing to the watercolors with construction-paper backings pinned on the wall.

"The calendar," Daria said, pointing to the calendar.

"The doors," Queenie said, pointing to the cupboard doors.

After doing this for the other shapes, Leyani introduced three different activities for the children to do, setting them up at three different locations in the room. On one table, she placed a set of blocks with shapes similar to the shapes in the book—several sizes of squares, rectangles, triangles, and diamonds (parallelograms). She also set out blank paper, one sheet at each place available for children to work. "When you go to this table," Leyani said to introduce the activity, "you put blocks on your paper to make a picture. When I come to see you at work, I'll ask you to tell me what you've made. After you make a picture, you can put the blocks back in the pile and make another." (**Note:** You can do this activity with any sets of blocks you may have—pattern blocks, attribute blocks, marquetry blocks, etc.)

Leyani placed the copy of *The Shape of Things* on another table. "When you come here," she told the children, "one person opens the book to a page and tells what the shape is. Then all of you look around the room for examples of where you see that same shape."

Leyani then described the third activity. This was the only activity for which the children would produce a permanent product. "On this table," she said, "there are lots of cutout paper shapes." Leyani had cut triangles, rectangles, circles, and squares from construction paper, each about the same size as the shapes shown on the left-hand pages in the book. "You pick any one shape, paste it on your paper, and then make a picture out of it. You can use the ideas you saw in the book, or you can use your own ideas."

Leyani then organized the children into three groups and had them rotate to the three activities, spending about ten minutes at each. The children were used to working at stations in this way and the activities went smoothly. Leyani circulated and talked with the children about what they were doing.

At the table with the blocks, Deandra said, "I made a sun and a lollipop."

Danny explained his construction. "This is a house," he said.

"I did a house, too," Mallika said.

At the table with the paper shapes, Tamera used a rectangle as the roof on a house, Fawziya used a triangle as the roof on a house, Rico pasted down a square for a house and drew a triangular roof on it, and Mallika used a rectangle for a house. (See Figures 13–1 and 13–2.) Mansur chose a triangle and made a fish. "This is the tail and this is a bubble," he said to describe his picture.

Eduardo used a circle to make a car, Acacia used a circle as the head of his dad, and Gamila drew a picture of herself using a circle for her head. "My eyes are circles, too," she said. (See Figures 13–3 and 13–4.)

Figure 13–1: Mallika pasted down a rectangle for a house and drew a triangle on top for the roof.

*Math and Literature, Grades K–1*

To follow up the experience, Leyani gathered the children again. "I'm going to show all of the pictures you did, but I'm not going to hold them up the right way. I'll either hold them upside-down or sideways." The children giggled at this idea. "I'll flip through your pictures quickly, and for each one, tell me what shape you see. I don't want to hear 'house' or 'boy' or 'girl.' Instead, I want to hear 'square,' 'triangle,' 'circle,' or 'rectangle.'" Showing the pictures in different positions helps children identify shapes even when the shapes are oriented differently than they are typically presented.

Figure 13–2: Fawziya used a triangle to show a roof on her house.

Figure 13–3: Gamila did a self-portrait using a circle for her head.

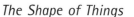

Figure 13–4: Deandra explained her picture. She said, "I made me right there and my name."

*Math and Literature, Grades K–1*

# Six-Dinner Sid

*Taught by Stephanie Sheffield*

*Six-Dinner Sid* is a charming story by Inga Moore (1991) about Sid, an enterprising young cat who lives on Aristotle Street. Sid has convinced six people on the street that each is his owner and therefore goes to six different houses and gets six different dinners every night. When the neighbors catch on and make sure that Sid only has one dinner a day, Sid moves to a new neighborhood, to Pythagoras Place. Stephanie Sheffield reads the book to first graders in this lesson and gives them the problem of determining how many dinners Sid eats in one week.

## MATERIALS

Stephanie gathered her first-grade class on the rug. Before she showed the students the cover of *Six-Dinner Sid*, she told them that she thought they would be excited to see the main character. She pointed to the board that held the graph the class had made the day before, which showed their favorite animals.

"Cats!" Nina shouted. Stephanie displayed the cover of the book so that the students could see that Sid was indeed a cat.

This was the beginning of the year, and Stephanie was encouraged when Eddie read the word *Six* in the title. Stephanie read the entire title, and Kimberly immediately noticed and counted the stack of six bowls in the picture. Stephanie had the children predict from the cover what the story would be about, and then she read it to them.

The children enjoyed the story. As Stephanie read, Cal pointed out the pages that had six pictures divided in different ways. "Three and three makes six," he said when he saw the picture of Sid eating out of six different bowls.

When Stephanie finished the book, the class talked about the differences between the two neighborhoods. Stephanie asked whether Sid really needed six dinners every night.

"We only feed our cat once a day," Nina said.

"I think he's going to get fat," added Harlan.

Next, Stephanie posed a question. She asked, "How many dinners do you think Sid ate in a whole week?"

"Six," Amy answered right away.

"No," Timothy said, "he had six just in one day."

"Oh yeah," Amy agreed.

"How many days are there in a week?" Stephanie asked. The class had been working with the calendar each day, and the children answered "Seven" in unison. Stephanie told them that they would need to use this information to answer her question about the number of dinners Sid ate in a week.

"Who can tell the question I asked?" Stephanie said. She usually asks several students to restate a problem. Restating a problem seems to help children understand and remember it. Also, having several children restate the problem gives students the opportunity to hear the question several times and in different ways. She called on a few volunteers to give the question.

Next, Stephanie told the students what she expected from them. "I'm going to give each of you a sheet of blank paper," she said. "I'd like you to try to find the answer to the question, then write words or numbers or draw pictures to help me understand how you got your answer. You may use any materials in our room that you think will help you. When I read your papers later, I want to be able to tell what you used and what you did. You can work alone or with a partner."

Stephanie then asked students to suggest some of the materials they thought might be helpful to them. Mary suggested Snap Cubes, and other children mentioned beans, links, and tiles. "Any of these might be helpful," Stephanie said, "but you should think about how you will use the materials before taking them off the shelves."

Before Stephanie had the students return to their seats and begin to work, she asked if anyone had questions. Sharon raised her hand.

"How do you spell *dinner*?" she asked.

"I'll write it on the board," Stephanie said. On the board she wrote: *Sid had _____ dinners in a week*. "You may copy this and use it on your paper if you want."

Stephanie distributed paper, and the children began to work. As Stephanie walked around, it was easy to tell who had an idea and who was still struggling with the question. She stopped at Eddie's desk. He was busily making trains with six Snap Cubes in each.

"Why are you making trains of six?" Stephanie asked.

"Because Sid had six dinners every day," he responded.

"Which day does this represent?" Stephanie asked, pointing to one of the groups.

"What does *represent* mean?" Eddie asked.

"It means 'stands for,'" Stephanie replied. "Which day does this group of cubes stand for?"

"Sunday," he told her. As she pointed to groups of cubes, Eddie named the days of the week. He was surprised when he reached the last group and said, "Friday." He had thought he had enough for the entire week.

"Did I already count that one?" he asked, pointing to one of the trains.

"I think so, but why don't you count again to be sure?" Stephanie answered. Eddie repeated the days of the week as he pointed to each train. Then he reached for the bag of cubes.

"I need another one for Saturday," he told Stephanie.

Stephanie left Eddie and looked around the room to see how others were doing. She noticed that Craig was also making trains with six Snap Cubes in each. Russell was making a long chain of links, using six of one color and then six of another. Ronnie had pattern blocks on her desk and was happily fitting them together to make designs. She seemed not to be considering the problem at all. Stephanie decided to give her a few minutes and check on her then.

Kimberly raised her hand to call Stephanie over to her desk. She had arranged popcorn kernels into groups of six and was excited to show them to Stephanie. Stephanie asked her why she did this, and she just smiled and shrugged her shoulders.

Stephanie finds that early in the year, first graders often have good ideas and good problem-solving abilities but are limited in their ability to verbalize their thinking. That's why she thinks it is so important to ask them to explain their thinking. It pushes them to describe the mental processes they are using.

Kimberly found it difficult to describe what she had done. When Stephanie questioned her, she was quickly willing to abandon her idea, as if it must be wrong if her teacher was asking about it. Stephanie assured her that she had great ideas but that Stephanie wanted to hear her talk about them. Even as early as first grade, children sometimes get the message that teachers ask them to explain their thinking only when they have wrong answers.

Stephanie used a series of questions to probe Kimberly's thinking: "What's the question I asked you to think about? Why did you make piles of six popcorn kernels? How many piles did you make? Why?" The questions helped Kimberly explain what she had done. Her

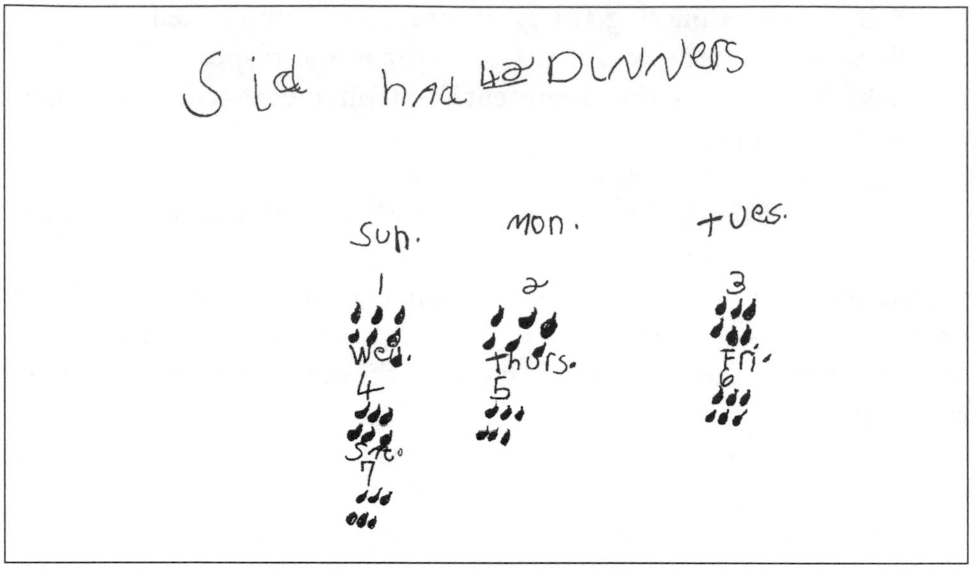

Figure 14–1: Kimberly made groups of popcorn kernels to find the answer.

Sid had 40 DINNers

Sun.        mon.        tues.

1           2           3

Wed.        thurs.      Fri.

4           5           6

Sat.

7

answers revealed to Stephanie that she understood the problem and her solution. Stephanie asked her to record her answer on paper.

"Can I draw pictures of the popcorn?" Kimberly asked.

"That would be fine," Stephanie told her. She noticed later that Kimberly had turned her desk to face the calendar and was copying abbreviations for the days of the week to label her picture. (See Figure 14–1.)

Nina, Sharon, and Audrey were sitting together with cubes scattered on their desks. They seemed to be working together, but they were having difficulty deciding what to do with the cubes. Stephanie approached and asked what they were doing. They seemed confused, so she asked them to restate the problem, a task that was difficult for them. In the minutes since leaving the rug, they had lost their focus on the problem and were now exploring the cubes, making patterns and trains the way the class had been doing for several weeks. Stephanie talked about the story and asked the question again, "How many dinners did Sid eat in a week?"

None of these girls seemed able to begin thinking about this question. Stephanie talked with them about the days of the week and the number of dinners Sid ate each day, but still the girls were confused and frustrated. Stephanie decided to let them return to their pattern building and made a note to herself about this discussion. Since her purpose in this activity was to give students a problem and assess their problem-solving strategies, she didn't feel it was necessary to push them to the point of frustration.

She continued walking around the room, making notes to herself about how students were working. She noted who chose to work with a partner and who worked alone. She watched to see which children used manipulatives effectively on their desks but couldn't translate their thinking to paper. This is very common at the beginning of the year, and often those students need encouragement to draw pictures of what they've done.

Stephanie then went back to watch what Ronnie was doing with the pattern blocks. To Stephanie's surprise, she was lining up rows of six of each shape and tracing around them. She had also drawn a picture of a cat at the bottom of the page. Stephanie was reminded that children often just need time to work out their own solutions. Ronnie was a quiet child who sometimes had trouble expressing herself and became frustrated. Stephanie was glad she hadn't intervened earlier.

Although this was a fairly difficult problem for first graders early in the school year, Stephanie learned a good deal about her students by observing them grapple with it. She learned that some of them needed more time exploring the materials, while others were already comfortable using materials to solve a problem. She discovered that some children preferred to work alone, yet continually check in with others for reassurance that they were on the right track. She learned about the frustration levels of a few and the confidence of others. She didn't worry too much about children's answers, but she noted which children seemed concerned about getting the right answer and which didn't.

This problem allowed Stephanie's class to think about numbers in a new way, to use manipulatives to represent large numbers, and to practice recording their ideas on paper. And for her it was a useful assessment tool. (Figure 14–2 shows how Russell worked on this activity.)

Figure 14–2: Russell made a group of six for each day of the week. However, he miscounted, and his answer was off by one.

# Ten Black Dots

*Taught by Marge Genolio*

In *Ten Black Dots*, Donald Crews (1995) uses black dots in colorful illustrations of everyday objects. He begins with one dot and continues up to ten dots, with a different number on each spread and a simple rhyme describing what the dots make. In this lesson, Marge Genolio presents this book near the end of the school year to her first graders and engages the children first in making pages for their own versions of the book, over several days, and then in a problem-solving activity. Marge got the idea for the activity from Olga Torres, who introduced the book to another class of first graders.

## MATERIALS

$\frac{3}{4}$-inch black adhesive dots, 2 packages of 1,000 each (or enough for each student to have 55 dots)

Donald Crews begins *Ten Black Dots* by posing the question "What can you do with ten black dots?" The book then shows 1 dot and illustrates how it can make a sun or a moon, and then 2 dots as the eyes of a fox or eyes of keys. It continues with 3, 4, 5, 6, 7, 8, 9, and 10 dots, using the dots to represent different objects on each page—beads, knobs, buttons, portholes, wheels, pennies, balloons, and more.

Marge read the book several times to her first-grade class. As the children became more familiar with the book, they enjoyed predicting what the dots would next represent. Also, on each page, Marge had the children count along with her as she pointed to the dots. For example, for the number five, she first read the text on one side of the spread about five dots making buttons on a coat and then had the children count to five as she pointed to the buttons in the illustration. She did the same for the other side of the spread, where the dots represent portholes of a boat. Finally, she pointed out the numeral 5 and the word *five* to reinforce the connection.

After these readings, Marge asked, "What ideas do you have about things that dots could make?" Marge gave all of the children who had ideas the opportunity to share them.

"They can be wheels," Aaron said.

"They can be eyes," Maria said. "Or faces," she added.

"They can be balloons," Hiroshi said.

"Buttons," Camilla said.

"I think like Aaron said, they can be wheels," William shared.

Then Marge presented the activity she had planned. "Now you'll each get to make your own pages for a *Ten Black Dots* book," Marge said. She showed the students the paper they would use for their books—newsprint with an unlined top portion for illustrations and a lined bottom portion for the children's writing.

Marge continued with the directions. "You'll use a different sheet of paper for each number from one to ten," she said. "On the top part of the page, you'll draw one idea for what the dots could be. Then you will write about what the dots made on the bottom of the page. I'll write sentence starters to help you." Marge turned to the board and wrote a sentence starter for each page.

*One dot can make* _____.
*Two dots can make* _____.
*Three dots can make* _____.
*Four dots can make* _____.
*Five dots can make* _____.
*Six dots can make* _____.
*Seven dots can make* _____.
*Eight dots can make* _____.
*Nine dots can make* _____.
*Ten dots can make* _____.

"How many pages will you make for your book?" Marge asked. Some of the children knew instantly that they would make ten pages; others counted the sentence starters, some keeping track on their fingers.

Marge continued, "After you have an idea for a page, draw a picture that shows where the dots should go. Then bring your page to me and tell me what you're going to write." Marge showed the children two packages of $\frac{3}{4}$-inch black adhesive dots. "I bought these dots in a stationery store for you to use for your pages," she explained. "After you show me your drawing, I'll give you dots and you'll carefully peel them off and place them on your drawing." The children were interested and eager to begin.

"You won't have time to do all of your pages today," Marge added. "You'll work on them over the next several days."

It took almost two weeks for all of the children to finish their books. As children finished each drawing, Marge would give them a page of dots with the request, "Take just the number you need and then bring the page back to me." In this way, she was able to keep track of the dots and focus their use just on the children's pages.

When Carla was ready for dots for her page for the number eight, Marge first gave her a sheet that had only three dots left on it. "How many more dots do you need for your page?" she asked.

Carla thought for a moment and then responded confidently, "Five."

Marge questioned other children in the same way, using the distribution of dots as an informal assessment. All of the students weren't as confident as Carla. Some pointed to the dots showing and then counted on to the number they needed, keeping track on their fingers; others didn't have a way to figure.

Most of the students completed one or two pages each day, keeping their finished pages in their folders. Marge gave some time each day for the students to work on their books; some students also worked on them when they completed other assignments or had time for free choice. When a student completed ten pages, Marge stapled them into a book and set it aside. After all the books were done, over several more days, the children shared what they had created. (See Figures 15–1 through 15–3.)

Figure 15–1: Maria used the dots as the faces of nine rabbits.

*Math and Literature, Grades K–1*

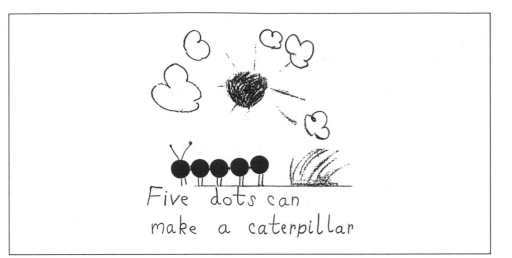

Figure 15–2: Alice used five dots for the body of a caterpillar.

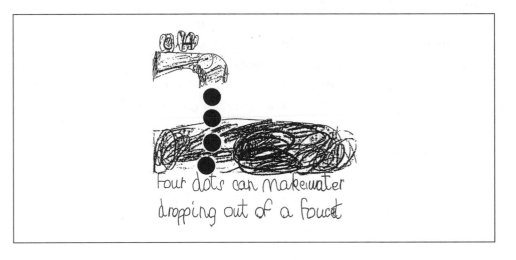

Figure 15–3: William drew a faucet and used four dots to show the water.

## A Follow-up Activity

After all the children had presented their work, Marge presented them with a problem to solve. She showed the class the remaining sheets of dots from the two packages she had bought. "These are the dots we have left over," she said. "When the packages were full, each had one thousand dots in it. How many dots did we have in the two packages together?"

"Two thousand," Isaac answered.

Marge responded, "Yes, we had two thousand dots when we started—one thousand dots plus one thousand dots equals two thousand dots." Marge held up each package in turn as she said this.

"How many dots do you think we used to make our books?" Marge then asked the children. Some children guessed. Others had no idea. One child suggested they could use a calculator to find out, and many of the others thought that was a good idea.

Marge said, "Let's start by each of you figuring out how many dots you used to make your own book. I'll give you paper to record your thinking, but you can use any materials you'd like to help you figure out the answer." To help the children in reporting their results, Marge wrote on the board:

*We each needed ___ dots. I got my answer by _____.*

She then said, "Copy what I've written on your paper and fill in the first line with your answer. Then, where I drew the second line, explain your reasoning."

Nine of the children arrived at the correct solution of fifty-five. Their explanations, however, differed. Carla, for example, wrote: *I got my answer by 1 + 2 + 3 + 4 + 5 + 6 + 7 + 8 + 9 + 10 = 55.* On her paper, Linda drew squares to represent the dots, making vertical columns of one, two, three, and so on, up to ten. Then she counted them. She wrote: *I got my answer by couing* [counting]. Keenahn wrote: *I got the answer by counting the dots in my book.* Diana used Unifix cubes to represent the dots. She wrote: *I got my answer by unfix qub.* Adam drew tally marks, first drawing one, then two, then three, and so on. He carefully organized them into groups of five. Then he wrote: *I got my answer by uozing tale-maks.* (See Figures 15–4 through 15–6.)

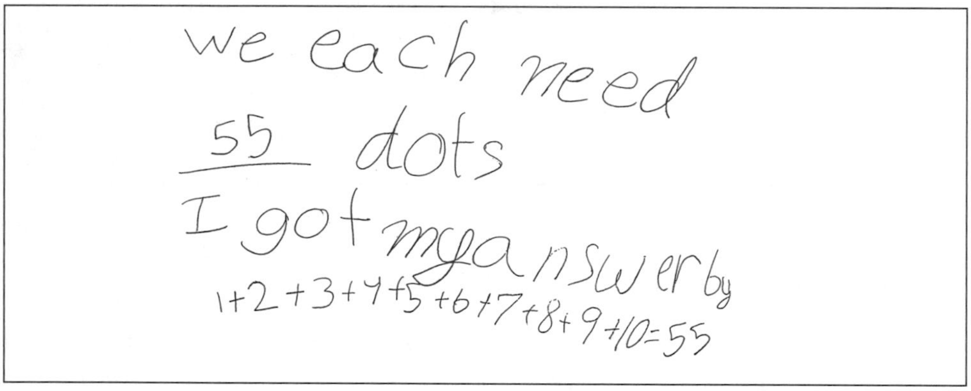

Figure 15–4: Carla's solution showed her comfort with representing the problem numerically.

Figure 15–5: Linda's drawing helped her figure out the number of dots each child needed.

*Math and Literature, Grades K–1*

*(handwritten)* We each needed 55 dots
I got my answer by uozing tale-maks.

Some children used reasonable approaches but got the wrong answer because of a calculation error. William, for example, drew tally marks in orderly clusters, beginning with one tally mark and continuing to ten. He didn't group them by fives as Adam had. He left out a cluster of seven dots and also miscounted what he drew. He wrote: *We each needed 38 dots.* Shirley added the numbers from one to ten and got an answer of fifty. Stephanie drew pictures of the dots in a carefully arranged pyramid and reported: *We each need 53.* Nicole also got an answer of fifty-three. She wrote: *I got my answer by used unafix xubes.*

For some children, the numbers were too confusing. Lety wrote: *We think we need 19 dots because we need more than ten. When we were on the eight page we had more then ten.* Michala wrote: *We each needed 15. I gastht* [guessed]. Kenneth wrote: *We each needed 10 dots.* He didn't offer any explanation.

For students who finished quickly and were interested in another challenge, Marge offered two problems—figuring how many dots were used altogether by everyone in the class or figuring how many dots were used by all the children at their table. Five children worked on the problem. Alice explained that she used a calculator. She wrote: *Our class needed 1540 dots. Our table needs 330 dots. I got my answer by yousing the caokyoulether.* Keenahn wrote: $55 \times 28 = 1540$. *Our clas needs 1540 dots.* $55 \times 6 = 330$. *Our table needs 330 dots. I got my answers by multeplying.*

The range of abilities in Marge's class was not unusual for a class of first graders or for a class at any grade level. A problem such as this one is useful for assessing what students can do with numbers and how they think. Students need many such problems to help develop number sense, learn ways to compute, and become aware that there are more ways than one to solve a problem.

# Ten Flashing Fireflies

*Taught by Leyani von Rotz*

*Ten Flashing Fireflies*, by Philemon Sturges (1995), is a two-way counting book that combines counting down from ten to one and counting up from one to ten. Mysterious and magical nighttime illustrations accompany the text about a girl and a boy who see ten flashing fireflies in the night sky and capture them one by one. After all ten fireflies are in the children's jar, their light begins to flicker and fade, so the children open the jar and watch them fly away, again one by one. For this lesson, after reading the book to a kindergarten class, Leyani von Rotz engages the children in thinking about combinations of ten. She also reads the book to a class of first graders and extends the activity to include recording number sentences.

(**Note:** The same activities described here for *Ten Flashing Fireflies* can be used with other similar children's books. Try them with *Ten Little Bears*, by Kathleen Hague [1999], or, near Halloween, with *Ten Timid Ghosts on a Christmas Night*, by Jennifer O'Connell [2002].)

### MATERIALS

*Ten Flashing Fireflies* **work mat,** 1 per student
 (see Blackline Master)
**cubes, tiles, or other counters,** 10 per student

## Sharing the Book with Kindergartners

Leyani gathered the kindergarten children on the rug to read aloud *Ten Flashing Fireflies*. She showed the children the cover of the book and asked them what they noticed.

"It's really dark!" Gamil said.

"There's a little boy, and he's holding something," Queenie said.

"It looks like a crystal ball," Deandra said.

"And there's another one over there, and there, and there," Fawziya said, pointing to each of the glowing spots on the cover.

Leyani said, "Let me read the title to you and see if that helps you think more about the picture. The title is *Ten Flashing Fireflies*."

Mallika said, "I remember when I was visiting my grandma there were fireflies at night and we'd try to catch them."

"Raise your hand if you've ever seen a firefly," Leyani said. A few hands shot up immediately, then a few others also raised their hands. Fireflies aren't common in the San Francisco Bay Area, where these children lived.

"Are they really on fire?" Mansur wanted to know.

Mallika, now the class expert on fireflies, responded in a matter-of-fact voice, "No, they're not on fire. But they have lights in them and they can light up to see where they are going."

"By themselves?" Kaisha asked, surprised. Conversation broke out among some of the other children.

Leyani asked for the children's attention. She could see their interest in fireflies growing, and she said, "This book doesn't tell us very much about fireflies. Later I'll help you learn more about them. But for now, I'd like to read this book to you and have you think about the story." Leyani waited for the children to settle down again and began to read.

Leyani read through the book. The children remained quiet and attentive, caught by the magical quality of the illustrations and the number pattern. Leyani then returned to the beginning of the book and read it again. This time, she stopped after reading the first page that introduces the ten flashing fireflies and had the children count the fireflies in the illustration as she pointed to them. The next spread shows one firefly in the jar, and Leyani had the children count to verify that there were nine still flying free. The following spread shows two in the jar, and as Leyani pointed to the ones still flying about, the children counted to eight. Leyani continued in this way until they got to the page on which all ten fireflies are shown in the jar and the boy and girl are about to go to bed.

"And what happened next in the story?" Leyani asked.

"They went to sleep," Acacia said.

"And the fireflies stopped making light," Bayard added.

"But then they let them go," Rico said.

Leyani read the remaining pages aloud, inviting the children at the end to count backward with her from ten down to one.

Leyani then explained to the children what they were going to do next. She showed them a work mat she had prepared with a picture of a jar on one side. She said, "In just a moment, I'm going to give each of you a work mat like this with a picture of a jar on it that's like the jar the girl and boy in the story used to keep the fireflies. And I'm going to give you each ten fireflies. They're really just cubes, but we're going to pretend that they are fireflies. Put your mat in front of you and then put your ten fireflies on the mat, but not in the jar. Put them all on the other side of the mat, the right side. Then I'll read the book again and you can act out what's happening on the mat with your own fireflies."

Leyani gave each child a mat and a train of ten interlocking cubes. As she did this, she said, "Take the cubes apart so the fireflies are all flying around the paper. But be sure that all of them are outside the jar." Leyani checked to be sure that all of the children did this correctly.

"How many fireflies are in the jar now?" Leyani asked.

Children had different answers. "None." "It's empty." "Zero."

"Yes, there are zero," Leyani said. Then she read the book again. Each time the children in the book put a firefly in the jar, Leyani had the kindergartners each move a cube into the jar on their mat. Next she read the first line from the facing page in the book: "What do we see in the summer night?" And then she asked, "And how many fireflies are still flying about?" She watched to see which children knew the answer immediately and which of them had to count. Also, she observed the children who counted to see if they did so correctly. Then Leyani read the rest of the text from the right-hand page, which revealed how many fireflies were still free, had the children check, and then continued. For example, after four fireflies were in the jar, Leyani read, "What do we see in the summer night? Six sparkling fireflies blinking bright." She asked the children to count again to be sure that there were six fireflies outside the jar on each mat. Then she continued reading, "Catch the one flying high. Now there are. . . ." Some children knew that next there would be five in the jar; others made a guess, some right and some wrong; others moved another cube into the jar and then counted. Then Leyani turned the page and read, "Five fiery fireflies in our jar."

After completing the second reading of the book, Leyani had the children count backward with her from ten down to one. This was easier for some children than for others. Counting backward calls for learning a new sequence and isn't easy for children, especially when their number understanding is still fragile.

## Sharing the Book with First Graders

Leyani also read the book to a class of first graders. When she reread the book, she asked the children to hold an imaginary jar in one hand and put imaginary cubes into it as the children in the story did. Doing the action, Leyani thought, would help prepare the children for what they would later do on their written assignment.

*Math and Literature, Grades K–1*

Also, Leyani drew a T-chart on the board. As she read, she kept track of the number of fireflies inside the jar and still flying about.

| In the Jar | Flying Free |
|:---:|:---:|
| 0 | 10 |
| 1 | 9 |
| 2 | 8 |
| 3 | 7 |
| 4 | 6 |
| 5 | 5 |
| 6 | 4 |
| 7 | 3 |
| 8 | 2 |
| 9 | 1 |
| 10 | 0 |

After finishing the book, Leyani asked, "What do you notice about the numbers on the chart?"

"They go up," Travis said.

"Which numbers go up?" Leyani asked.

"Those on that side," Travis said, pointing to the left-hand column. "See, they go zero, one, two, three, like that."

"And the other numbers go down," Jamila said.

"Let's read the numbers going down together," Leyani said, and she counted from ten to zero with the students.

Leyani then distributed a work mat and cubes to each of the first graders. She read the book again and had them move the fireflies just as she had done with the kindergartners. However, after the students had verified the number of fireflies still flying free on each page, Leyani recorded a number sentence on the board, showing the children another way to represent the story mathematically. By the end of the book, she had recorded eleven number sentences:

$$0 + 10 = 10$$
$$1 + 9 = 10$$
$$2 + 8 = 10$$
$$3 + 7 = 10$$
$$4 + 6 = 10$$
$$5 + 5 = 10$$
$$6 + 4 = 10$$
$$7 + 3 = 10$$
$$8 + 2 = 10$$
$$9 + 1 = 10$$
$$10 + 0 = 10$$

Leyani then pointed to one of the number sentences on the board—
2 + 8 = 10. "What was happening in the story when I wrote this
number sentence?" Leyani asked. She waited until more than half the
children had raised their hands and then called on several to explain.

"There were two in the jar and eight still flying," Natalie said.

"They had captured two and the other eight were free," Hassan
said.

"First they had one in the jar, but then they put another one in,
and now there were eight outside," Vincent explained.

Leyani repeated this question, asking about several of the other
number sentences. Then she gave the children an assignment to do
on their own. "Pick one of the number sentences from the board
and copy it onto your work mat," she said. "Then draw fireflies on
your mat to show what the sentence means." As the children
returned to their desks, Leyani circulated, helping several of the children get started with the assignment.

Some of the children focused on making detailed drawings of
fireflies while others merely drew dots or circles. Some children colored their drawings and others weren't interested in doing so. All but
three of the students completed the assignment correctly by themselves. Paulo miscounted and had only nine fireflies on his paper;
when Leyani pointed this out to him, he figured out the mistake he
had made. Cameron wrote the number sentence *0 + 10 = 0* but then
drew five fireflies in the jar and five outside. Cameron had difficulty
in general and was just learning the meaning of the numerals. Janelle
copied the sentence incorrectly, writing *8 + 10 = 2*, but she correctly
illustrated the sentence *8 + 2 = 10*. (See Figures 16–1 through 16–3.)

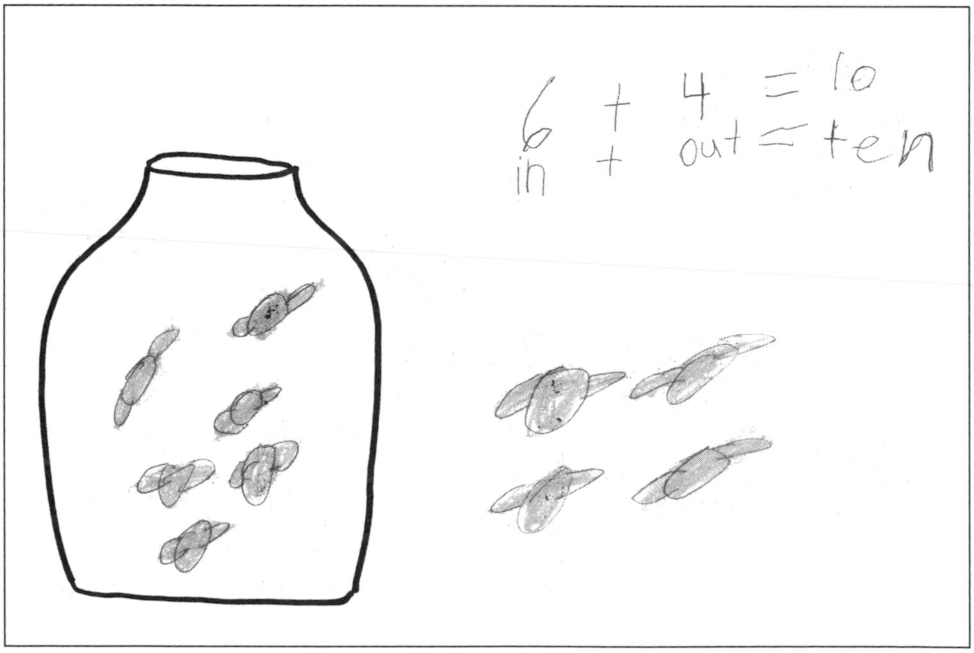

Figure 16–1: David illus-
trated 6 + 4 = 10 and then
wrote another sentence:
*in + out = ten*. He ex-
plained, "I wanted to do
words, too."

*Math and Literature, Grades K–1*

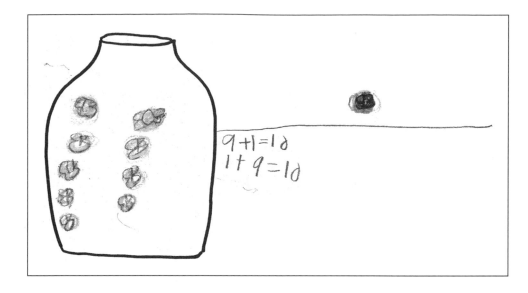

Figure 16–2: Jerilyn's two number sentences showed her understanding of the commutative property of addition.

Figure 16–3: Vincent illustrated 10 + 0 = 10. "I wanted them all in the jar," he said.

Leyani asked those children who finished quickly to repeat the activity for other sentences. Rather than give them additional work mats, however, Leyani had the children fold a sheet of paper into fourths. That way they could write a sentence in each section and then draw a jar and fireflies to illustrate it. (See Figure 16–4.)

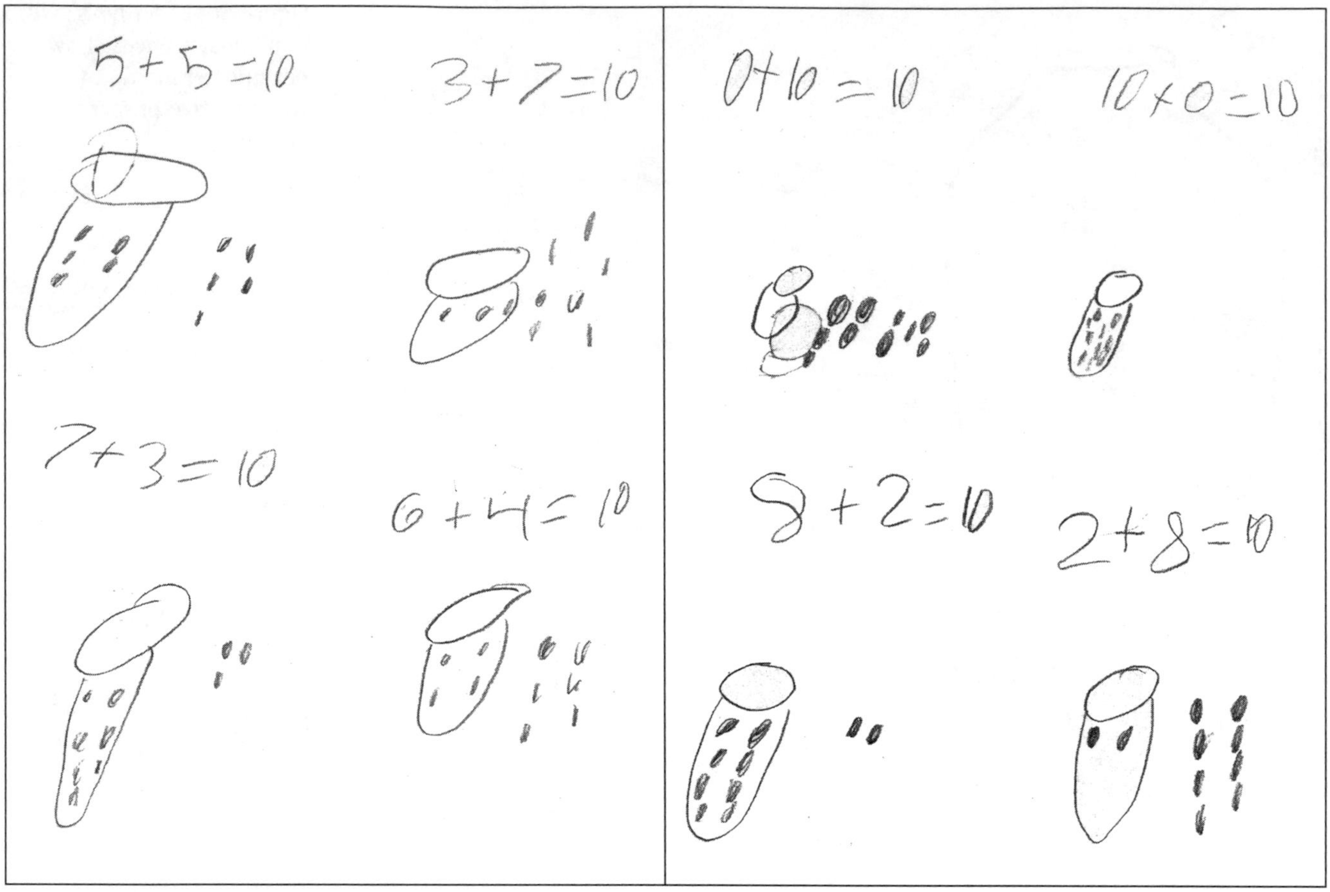

5 + 5 = 10          3 + 7 = 10          0 + 10 = 10              10 × 0 = 10

7 + 3 = 10
                    6 + 4 = 10          8 + 2 = 10      2 + 8 = 10

Figure 16–4: Travis had time to illustrate eight sentences.

# Ten Sly Piranhas

## Taught by Stephanie Sheffield

*Ten Sly Piranhas*, by William Wise (1993), is a counting book in reverse. It tells about ten piranhas that disappear one at a time. Nine become the victims of a greedy fellow piranha, who in turn becomes a meal for a crocodile. This book, while a bit grim in its premise, is rollicking in its cadence. The bright illustrations invite children into the river world of sly and cunning piranhas. Stephanie Sheffield reads the book to a first-grade class in this lesson and then leads a discussion about subtraction and writing subtraction number sentences.

**MATERIALS**

Before Stephanie read *Ten Sly Piranhas* to her class of first graders, she asked if anyone knew what piranhas were. Since the children were not familiar with these fish and their voracious habits, Stephanie told them a bit about piranhas. Using the large class atlas, the class located the Amazon River, where these fish live.

When Stephanie read the book, the children delighted in the rhythm of the words and the sneakiness of the greedy piranha. A few pages into the book, they began counting backward to predict the number of piranhas left. They watched with glee as one piranha got bigger and bigger, and the number of piranhas decreased. "Look out!" they yelled as they became aware of the pattern in the story and then chanted along, "And with a gulp and a gurgle—there were only eight." When Stephanie read the last sentence of the book,

"And so ends the story of those foxy little fishes—unless you'd like to hear it told the same way again," the resounding response was "Yes, read it again!" Stephanie was pleased to do so.

She then told the children she'd read the book a third time. "This time ten children will act out the story as I read," she said. She chose ten children and designated Kimberly to be the very hungry and crafty piranha who manages to eat all its fellow fish. As Stephanie read, Kimberly "swam" about, repeating the words the sly piranha used to trick its friends. After the first fish was eaten, Stephanie asked all the fish to stop moving for a minute.

"Let's talk about what just happened," she said. "How many piranhas were there to start with?"

"Ten!" the children responded. Stephanie asked Conner to record. He went to the board and wrote 10.

"How many fish were eaten?" Stephanie then asked.

After Conner recorded 1, several children chorused, "And how many piranhas were left?" Others responded, and Conner wrote 9.

"What kind of action took place on this page?" Stephanie asked.

"One piranha was eaten," Timothy said.

"Yes," Stephanie said. "Let's write a sentence to tell with numbers what happened. Which number should come first?" The children responded with ten, and Conner again wrote 10 on the board.

"What symbol do we use to show that something is being taken away from the group?" Stephanie asked.

"Minus," Sharon answered, "and we need an equal sign."

They continued in this way for the entire story, with the children telling Conner how to record numerically the action taking place in the story. This was not the first time the class had constructed number sentences to describe a situation the students were acting out. Connecting mathematical representations to actions helps children learn the meanings of mathematical symbols.

After Conner had recorded several equations on the board, Stephanie asked the students to take out their small chalkboards. Then, as she read, each child recorded a number sentence to represent the action while Conner continued writing on the board. As the classroom piranhas were eaten, they sat down and recorded on their chalkboards.

$$10 - 1 = 9$$
$$9 - 1 = 8$$
$$8 - 1 = 7$$
$$7 - 1 = 6$$
$$6 - 1 = 5$$
$$5 - 1 = 4$$
$$4 - 1 = 3$$

$$3 - 1 = 2$$
$$2 - 1 = 1$$
$$1 - 1 = 0$$

After the class finished reading the book, Stephanie asked the students to look for patterns in the number sentences. Mary raised her hand.

"These numbers are going down by one," she said, pointing to the first column of numbers.

"And so are these," Anita added, pointing to the answers.

"Why doesn't this number change?" Stephanie asked, indicating the 1 in each equation.

Timothy answered, "That's the one piranha that gets eaten every time."

This lesson was valuable for the students. It gave children the opportunity to connect the symbols we use in mathematics to a situation of interest to them. However, learning how symbols connect to situations comes only from repeated experiences over time. Children need many such opportunities to internalize the meaning of symbols such as the minus and equals signs.

# A Three Hat Day

*Taught by Bonnie Tank*

Laura Geringer's book *A Three Hat Day* (1985) is ideal to read to young children. Delightfully illustrated by Arnold Lobel, the book tells the story of R.R. Pottle the Third, a man who truly loves hats and has a wonderful collection, but who is also unhappy because he is lonely. However, his hats become the way to his happiness. In this lesson, Bonnie Tank reads the book to a class of first graders and then uses the story to involve the children in a problem-solving math lesson.

## MATERIALS

Bonnie gathered the first graders to the rug to hear the story about R.R. Pottle, who comes from a family of collectors. His father collected canes and his mother liked umbrellas. Together they took long walks in the rain. Now that his parents are no longer alive, R.R. Pottle lives alone. At times, however, he is very lonely. One day, to cheer himself up, he puts on three of his hats—a bathing cap, a fire helmet, and a sailor hat—and goes for a walk.

On his walk, R.R. happens upon a hat store and makes the acquaintance of the woman who owns it. Their common interest in hats draws them together. They fall in love, get married, and have a child, R.R. Pottle the Fourth. (It turns out that R.R. Pottle the Fourth doesn't like hats, umbrellas, or canes. She loves shoes.)

After reading the story, Bonnie gave time for the children to share their thoughts.

"He was sad when he lived alone," Lisa said.

"But then the lady made him happy again," Daniel commented.

"I like how he wore all three hats at one time," Luis said.

"I have a fireman's hat," Todd said. "I was a fireman for Halloween."

"I have a cowboy hat," Leslie said.

"The lady in the store was mean," Laura said. She was referring to the clerk in the hat store who was angry with R.R. Pottle for trying on hats and doing a jig. This was before the owner of the store, his future bride, came out from behind a curtain.

After all of the children who wanted to had shared their ideas, Bonnie asked, "Which hat did R.R. Pottle put on first?" She showed the children the cover illustration from the book, and the children were able to figure out that R.R. had first put on the bathing cap, then the fire helmet, and finally the sailor hat.

Bonnie then presented a problem for the children to solve. "Suppose R.R. Pottle wanted to cheer himself up on another day with the same three hats," Bonnie said, "but he decided to put on the hats in a different order. And then the next day he put them on in a different order again. The problem for you to solve is to figure out how many days R.R. Pottle could wear those same three hats if each day he wanted to wear them in a different order."

Bonnie talked to the children about how they were to work. "You'll each work with a partner," she said. "Think about what can help you solve the problem. You may want to use cubes for the hats, you may want to use pictures, or you may decide that symbols are helpful. What do I mean by 'symbols'?"

Some of the children had ideas. "Like a drawing?" Robert asked.

"Yes, that's one idea," Bonnie answered. "Does anyone have another idea?"

"Maybe letters," Kimberly said.

"That's another idea," Bonnie said. "What letter might you use for the fire helmet?" In unison, several children suggested F. They talked about using B and S for the other two hats.

When they got to work, all the children were engaged in solving the problem. Most of them made drawings of the hats, and some of them also drew R.R. Pottle. Some children, after drawing hats for a few options, decided that drawing took too much time and switched to using letters for the hats. One pair of boys used numbers for the hats, assigning the number 1 to the bathing cap, 2 to the sailor hat, and 3 to the fire helmet. Several children began by ruling their paper into sections, planning to show a different way in each. Others didn't make any prediction about how many ways there might be and just began listing. All of the children proceeded by trial and error; no one worked in a systematic way. This is typical for children this age.

The problem seemed just right for the first graders—challenging, interesting, and possible. (Figures 18–1 through 18–4 show how several students worked on this activity.)

Figure 18–1: Laura and Sammy used drawings to represent their solution.

he can where all of these hats in six days.

Figure 18–2: Kimberly and Joanna started by drawing hats and then switched to symbols.

It was 6 days

*Math and Literature, Grades K–1*

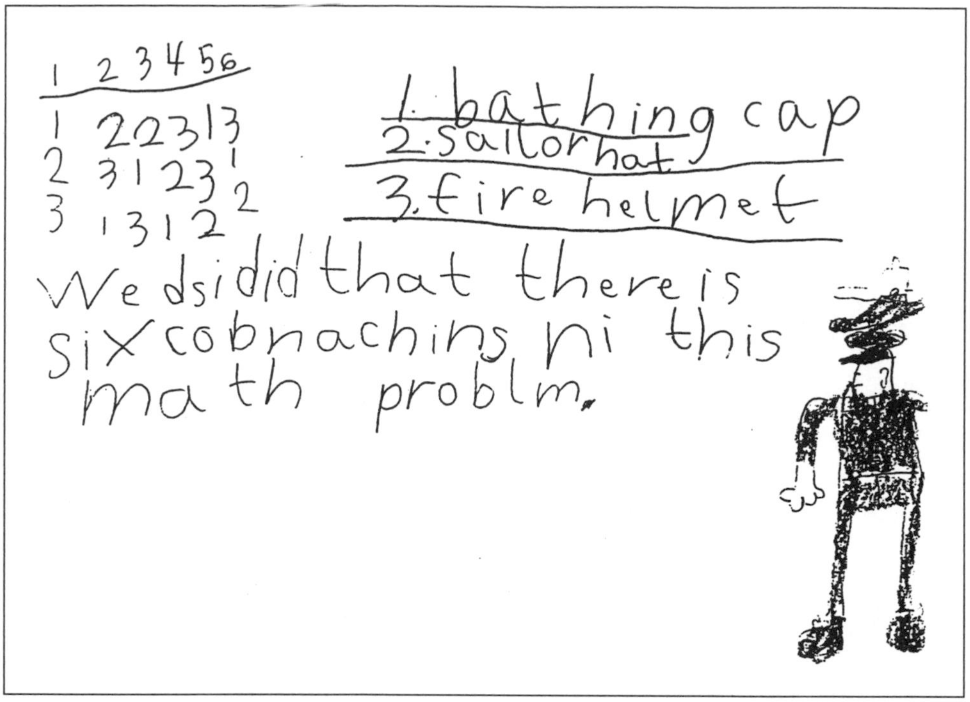

```
  1 2 3 4 5 6
1  2 2 3 1 3
2  3 1 2 3 1
3  1 3 1 2 2
```

1. bathing cap
2. sailor hat
3. fire helmet

We dsidid that there is six cobnachins ni this math problm.

Figure 18–3: Robert and Tim defined their numerical code for the hats.

We got 5 wh

Figure 18–4: Thayer and Ashleigh drew portraits of R. R. Pottle, each with a different arrangement of hats.

*A Three Hat Day*          **111**

# 12 Ways to Get to 11 and Band-Aids

*Taught by Stephanie Sheffield and Min Hong*

In *12 Ways to Get to 11,* Eve Merriam (1993) combines different objects to make groups of eleven. Nine pinecones from the forest floor and two acorns, one sow and ten baby piglets, and three sets of triplets and a pair of twins are a few of the combinations of items that add up to eleven. Colorful, bold illustrations make this book especially appealing to children. For this lesson, Stephanie Sheffield reads the book to a first-grade class and uses it a stimulus to discuss other combinations that total eleven.

Shel Silverstein's poem "Band-Aids," from *Where the Sidewalk Ends* (1974), is about a child who gets a little overzealous with Band-Aids and ends up plastered with them. Min Hong reads the poem to a first-grade class in this lesson and uses it as a springboard for the children to create number sentences. Then she reads *12 Ways to Get to 11* to the class and engages them in writing more number sentences and creating a class book.

## MATERIALS

chart paper, 2 sheets

library pocket, 1 per pair of students

3-by-5-inch index cards, 1 per pair of students

Stephanie showed the cover of *12 Ways to Get to 11* to her first graders and asked them if they knew how to count to eleven. The answer was a resounding "Yes!" and they all counted easily to eleven.

Then she asked, "Do you know any other ways to count to eleven?" They tried counting by twos and fives but decided that they couldn't get to eleven either way.

Stephanie opened the book and showed them the title page, which has the words and the numerals for eleven and twelve on it. The copyright page displays the numbers 1 to 10 and 12 across the top, with the number 11 on the bottom as if it has fallen out of sequence. The class talked about why the illustrator may have drawn them that way.

"It looks like eleven is missing," Shannon noticed, but then she spotted it at the bottom. The next page shows the words for the numbers one through twelve, but it has only a blank line where eleven should be.

"See," Shannon said, "I told you it was missing." The following page shows a black magician's hat and the words, *Where's eleven?*

Stephanie read the first page aloud: "Pick up nine pinecones from the forest floor and two acorns." Some of the children knew that nine and two make eleven, and some counted on their fingers, but all of them realized they had found the eleven on that page. The same was true for the next page, which shows six peanut shells and five pieces of popcorn.

But the third page was more of a challenge because four different things are put together to make eleven: "four banners, five rabbits, a pitcher of water, and a bouquet of flowers."

Many students listened to the rest of the book without doing more figuring, although a few continued to try to keep up on their fingers as Stephanie read. She didn't make an effort during this first reading to focus on the combinations; she just wanted the children to enjoy the book.

When Stephanie got to the end of the book, she asked the children if they were sure there were really eleven things on each page. They seemed to accept that there were, simply because of the name of the book, but Stephanie pushed them anyway.

"How could we be sure that eleven objects are on each page?" she asked.

"Count them," several children said.

Stephanie asked Drew to go to the board and be the record keeper. As Stephanie read the book again, Drew wrote the numbers that appeared on each page. For the first page, he wrote: *9 2.*

"It looks to me as if something is missing," Stephanie said, "because when I read what's on the board, it says, 'nine . . . two.'

To make eleven, we have to say, 'nine and two.' What symbol means 'and' in math?"

"Plus," Ramon said. "You need to put a plus between the nine and the two." Drew wrote a plus sign, and they continued.

After Stephanie finished reading, she reviewed what Drew had recorded. To give the children practice with mental arithmetic, she had them add aloud to figure out the total for each combination. Stephanie led the practice, saying, for example, "Four plus five is nine, plus one is ten, plus one is eleven." Many of the students kept up with her, and the children who couldn't at least had the opportunity to hear the sums as they looked at the numbers.

Michaela had a suggestion about the number combinations Drew had recorded: "We should add 'equals eleven' to them," she said. Stephanie asked her to come up and do so.

Then Stephanie asked the students if they thought there might be more ways to make eleven. "Talk with your neighbor," she said, "and see if you can come up with any other ways that aren't already on the board."

Some students suggested new combinations. "How about two plus two plus two plus two plus two plus one?" suggested Jessica.

"We could put one plus one plus one, and keep going until we get to eleven," Jack said.

Kendra suggested, "Three plus three plus three plus two."

However, when Shelly and Melanie reported 6 + 5, Jack noticed that they had merely rearranged the order of a combination already on the board. The class decided that since the order was different, it could be counted as a new combination.

After all of the students had reported their combinations, Stephanie wondered aloud whether they had them all. Hassan said he thought there might be a few more. Many children, like Renee, were unsure. Stephanie copied the combinations onto a chart, posted it on the wall, and encouraged the children to find new combinations to add.

## A Different Lesson in First Grade

Before Min Hong read *12 Ways to Get to 11* to her first-grade class, she thought the children needed an introduction to the idea that a sum could be made by adding more than two numbers. She chose to use Shel Silverstein's poem "Band-Aids," which begins: "I have a Band-Aid on my finger, One on my knee, and one on my nose. . . ." The poem continues with different numbers of Band-Aids elsewhere on the body.

Min wrote the poem on a chart and used it during shared reading time. She had the class read it together as a choral reading. And, as first graders often do with their favorite literature, it wasn't long before the students had memorized it.

After using the poem for several days during language time, Min asked her class, "How do you think this poem relates to math?" At first the children didn't see the poem as mathematical at all because the numbers in the poem were not written as numerals. When they reread the poem, however, they realized that the numbers were written as words. They had many ideas about what Min had in mind for them to do with this poem.

Feta said, "We're going to add all the Band-Aids."

"We're going to practice using calculators," Ramona said.

"What do you mean?" Min asked.

"Well, there are so many numbers to add, we'll need a calculator," she replied.

After listening to all their ideas, Min prepared them for the next part of the problem. She assigned each pair of children two lines of

Figure 19–1: Elizabeth copied the lines from the poem, wrote a math sentence to match, and also included an illustration.

the poem at random. The children had to read the lines and write a number sentence that described the words. They could also choose to illustrate their two lines. Some children used cubes or other counters to model the numbers in their lines before writing the number sentence. (See Figures 19–1 and 19–2.)

When all the groups were ready, Min asked the students to come together to share their papers. At one point, the children thought Min had made a mistake and given two groups the same lines of the poem because two pairs had the same sum for their number sentences. Min had the two groups with the same sum go to the board and write their number sentences. It was a surprise to some of the students to see the different numbers that made up the sum.

The next day, Min brought out *12 Ways to Get to 11*. She read the book aloud twice for the children to enjoy. Then she read the book again, taking time for the class to create a number sentence for each page. She recorded their sentences on a sheet of chart paper. Min reported that at first some of the students' totals were not eleven. She didn't correct them right away, but waited until they realized that *a* meant one.

When Min read the fourth page of the book, Marika suddenly exclaimed, "Oh, they all equal eleven!"

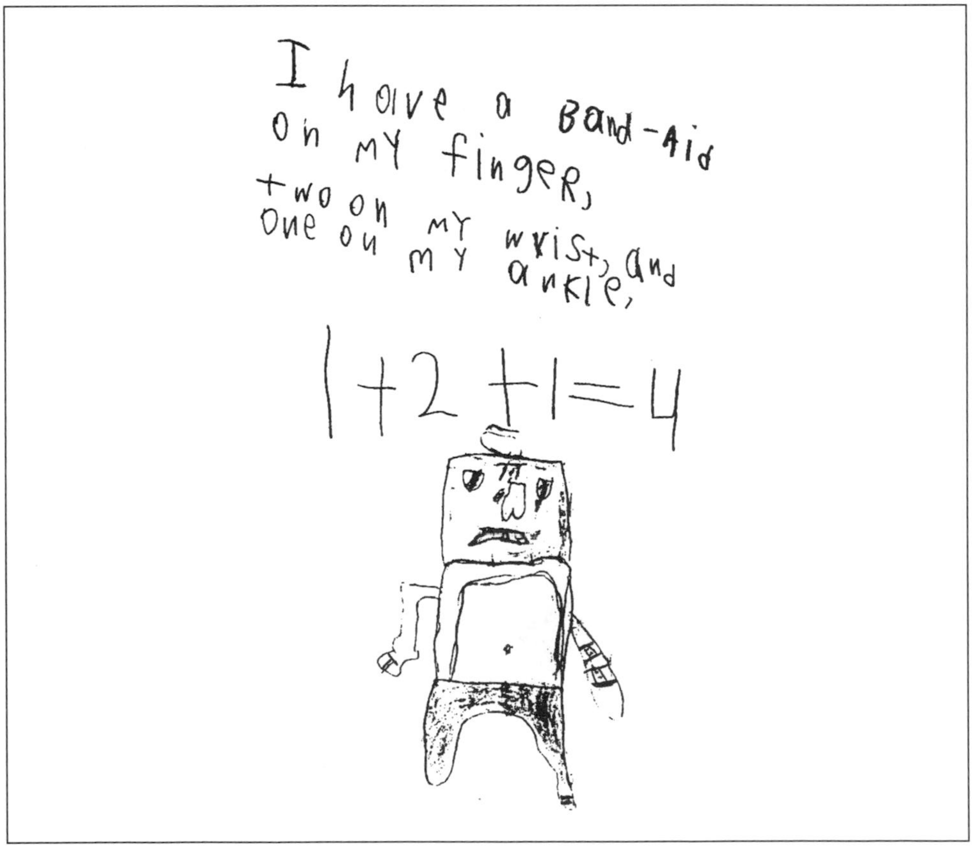

Figure 19–2: Feta wrote a math sentence and illustrated the two lines he was assigned.

*Math and Literature, Grades K–1*

Min reported: "From this point on, when the students counted the objects in the picture to write a number sentence, they didn't always get the addends right, but they always got the answer right." Min's classroom was culturally diverse, and for many of her students, English was not the language spoken at home. In several instances, the meanings of words became clear to these students as she read. One such word was *pair*. Students were pleased with themselves when they realized that *pair* meant two. "Many didn't know that before," Min said.

The following day, Min asked, "If we had to make our own book, what number would we choose as a sum?"

The class suggested twenty, fifty, and one hundred. Melissa said, "Well, why don't we do ten, because we always go to the number ten in math." The rest of the students nodded their approval.

Min posed another question. "We'll do 'blank' ways to get to ten. If we all pair up, how many ways will that be?" She allowed the children to think for a few minutes, then she paired them up and counted the pairs. "Our book's title will be *Thirteen Ways to Get to Ten*," she concluded.

Min asked each pair of children to write one page, describing a group of different things, and to be sure there were ten in all. "You'll also do an illustration for your page," she told them.

As the children started working, Min noticed that some of them started with the picture and added words later. Others began with the words, and still others wrote a number sentence first. Min circulated, observing the children and talking with them to be sure they had words and pictures that matched.

When all the students had completed at least part of the assignment, Min called them together to share. All the pairs showed what they had done so far, and the rest of the students offered helpful tips to make their pages better.

Lucas asked, "How will people know what the number sentence is if we don't tell them?" The children decided to make each page a game. Each pair put the words and the pictures on the front of the page and glued a library pocket on the back. They wrote their number sentence on a small index card and put it in the library pocket.

Before Min put the pages together to make a book, she decided to share the children's work with other students in the school. She posted the pages on the wall in the hall. Other students came by and tried to figure out the number sentences, then checked themselves by looking inside the library pockets. Her first graders were proud of their work and enjoyed watching older children read their book and solve their puzzles. (See Figures 19–3 and 19–4.)

Figure 19–3: Frank and
Adam chose a Halloween
theme.

+R WEre three jack-o-
lanterhns AND fiv monthal monkeys
and two bats at the
Halloween party.

$$3+5+2=10$$

Figure 19–4: Damon and
Emma wrote about super-
market items.

We went to the supermarcit and bot 4 orenges
2 apples and 4 Greyps.

$$4+2+4=10$$

# Two of Everything

*Taught by Stephanie Sheffield*

*Two of Everything*, by Lily Toy Hong (1993), is a Chinese folktale about an elderly couple who find magic right in their own backyard. Mr. Haktak discovers an ancient brass pot in his garden and decides to bring it to the house. He throws his coin purse into the pot for safekeeping. When Mrs. Haktak accidentally drops her hairpin in the pot and reaches in to get it, she pulls out two hairpins and two coin purses! Mr. and Mrs. Haktak realize their good fortune and get to work doubling their valuables. Stephanie Sheffield reads the book to first graders during this lesson and uses the book as a springboard to have the students investigate doubling numbers.

## MATERIALS

**chart paper,** 1 sheet

After reading *Two of Everything* to her first-grade class, Stephanie asked the students to explain what the pot did. This question was challenging because most of the children didn't have the vocabulary to answer precisely.

"Whatever went in came out again with another," Davy said.

Michaela said, "Yeah, it adds two each time."

But Jack and Branford quickly corrected her. "Five coins went in and ten came out," Jack said.

Branford added, "They didn't go from five to seven, like if they added two."

Finally Hassan spoke. He was a quiet boy who thought deeply about things. "I think it's doubling," he suggested.

119

"Yeah, that's right!" others chimed in. Although the class had talked about doubles in relation to adding, not all the students had transferred the word to this new situation. Stephanie reminded herself that children need to make connections for themselves.

Stephanie suggested that they write down some things that happened in the book so they could look at them. On chart paper, she drew a vertical line to make two columns, labeled the left column *In* and the right column *Out*, and drew a pot above. She wrote *5 coins* at the top of the left column.

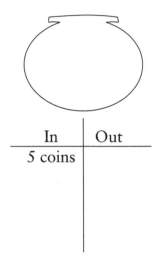

| In | Out |
|---|---|
| 5 coins | |

Stephanie asked the class, "If five coins went into the pot, what would come out?" Several students answered, and Stephanie wrote *10 coins* in the right column.

Next, she wrote *1 hairpin* in the left column and asked what should go next to it in the right column. When the children responded, she recorded *2 hairpins* in the right column.

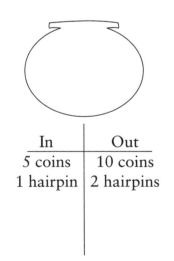

| In | Out |
|---|---|
| 5 coins | 10 coins |
| 1 hairpin | 2 hairpins |

Stephanie continued in this way, listing the other things from the book that went into and came out of the pot. Then she asked the children to think of something else that could fall into the pot. They suggested a chair, three pencils, and then the class soccer ball. Stephanie recorded each item and, after they talked about what would come out of the pot each time, she recorded that as well.

Stephanie then suggested a follow-up problem. She said, "Suppose we put a pair of shoes into the pot. How many pairs of shoes would have to go in so that everyone in our class would have shoes to wear?" This interested the children! Stephanie gave them time to talk to their neighbors. As she watched, she saw several of them looking around the room and counting students, some using their fingers.

After a few minutes, Stephanie asked for the children's attention and asked them to explain their thinking. She was interested to hear how they thought about the question.

Michaela said, "I counted by twos because everybody has two feet."

"How did you keep track as you were counting?" Stephanie asked.

"I pointed to people when I said the numbers," Michaela replied. "But I had to do it again, because I got mixed up and I didn't know if I counted Davy's feet already."

Michelle reported that she had done the same thing.

Jack offered, "I counted by twos, too, but I used my fingers."

"Show us how you did that," Stephanie said.

Jack held up his fists and showed just one finger and said, "Two." Each time he counted, he held up another finger. "My partner helped when I ran out of fingers," he told the class.

Although Stephanie expects students to listen to one another as they share, she sometimes finds that with children this age, she is the person most interested in what they have to say. It's difficult for first graders to articulate what they are thinking—and even more difficult for them to follow another student's line of reasoning.

Stephanie returned to talking about what else might fall into the pot. "What if half an apple fell into the pot?" she asked. Children disagreed about whether two halves or a whole apple would emerge.

"It's the same thing!" Jane exclaimed in an exasperated tone.

They considered more ideas, deciding as a class what should go in the second column for each. Dwight asked, "What if fifteen marbles fell in?"

Christa suggested, "I think three hair bows fell in."

When Branford asked what would happen if a pizza with eight slices fell in, Jessica replied, "You'd get two pizzas, but you'd have sixteen pieces!"

Then Stephanie reversed the question and asked, "What would have to fall into the pot in order for five dollars to come out?" The children were puzzled at first but then began to talk to one another.

"I think it's one dollar and . . . ," Kylie began, and she turned her eyes toward the ceiling as she thought. "No, it's got to be two dollars, because two and two is four."

"Then take half the other dollar and you get fifty cents," Hassan added. Hassan was sure about what he had said, but many children in the class didn't follow his thinking. As they discussed the question, Stephanie could tell which children had had experience with money at home.

"Let's try it out with real money," Michaela suggested. Stephanie dug into her wallet for bills and brought out the class jar of change. Michaela took charge. She took four bills and a dollar of change, divided it between Ramon and Shelly, and then counted it to prove her answer.

Over the next few days the class added items to the chart whenever a student came up with a new idea. Some of the items they added were a box of 16 crayons, a box of 24 crayons, 1 dozen eggs, and $50.00. Each time someone added an item to one side of the list, children rushed to figure out what to write on the other side.

# When a Line Bends . . . a Shape Begins

## *Taught by Leyani von Rotz*

Rhonda Gowler Greene's *When a Line Bends . . . a Shape Begins* (1997) provides an imaginative and effective introduction to shapes. Using rhymes and illustrations of familiar examples, the book starts with a line and then shows how it can bend to form ten different shapes—square, rectangle, triangle, diamond, circle, oval, star, heart, crescent, and octagon. In this lesson, Leyani von Rotz reads the book to kindergartners and first graders and then has them use pipe cleaners to make their own shapes.

## MATERIALS

**pipe cleaners,** at least 1 per student

Leyani gathered the kindergarten children on the rug to read aloud *When a Line Bends . . . a Shape Begins.* After reading the title, Leyani opened to the first page and read, "A line is thin. A line is narrow—curved like a worm, straight as an arrow."

Leyani then drew on the board several types of lines—straight, curved, wavy, and curly. While Leyani knew that the mathematical definition of a line is a set of points that forms a straight path, she wasn't interested at this time in introducing or focusing on this formal mathematical interpretation. Rather, her goal was to give the children experience thinking about how lines and curves can form different figures.

Leyani turned the page to reveal a spread of illustrations of lines. Before reading the text, Leyani asked the students to identify the examples of lines shown.

"The fishing pole," Jorge said, pointing to the boy in a boat.

"The worm's going like this," Hallie said, wiggling her finger.

"That's yucky," Kara commented.

"The kite has a line," Jesus said.

"Where do you see a line?" Leyani asked, not sure if Jesus meant the kite string or the lines drawn on the kite.

Jesus pointed and said, "There, the string going there."

After all the children who wanted to had a chance to share what they saw, Leyani read the text that identified a jump rope, black ants in a row, a tug-of-war game, the bow of a violin, a fishing pole, a leash, a kite string, a shoelace, and more. She again showed the children the illustrations and read the text, asking them to find each of the items mentioned. The children were interested in doing the search.

"Oh! The tail's all curly," Bobby said.

"I said the kite string!" Jesus said proudly.

"It's a U," Purna said, referring to the jump rope.

Leyani turned the page and showed the students the illustration of the circus performer bending a pipe into a circle.

Several students shouted, "It's a circle!"

"He's got muscles," Aaron said, holding up his arms to show his muscles.

Leyani turned the page and pointed to the large red square that was featured prominently on the left page. "What's this shape?" she asked the children.

"A square," they answered in unison.

Before reading the text, Leyani said, "Talk with your partner about the squares you see in the illustration." After giving the children a few moments to do this, she asked for volunteers to share their ideas.

"The squares make houses," Daniela said.

"The blocks," Danny said.

"The robot head," Mansur said.

"The hopscotch thing," Purna noticed.

"The cracker," Gamil said.

Leyani then read the text and, as she did after reading the text about the lines, she asked the children to identify the items listed.

The next spread presents a rectangle, and Leyani again first asked the children to find examples of rectangles, then read the text, and then asked them to locate the items described.

After reading the page about rectangles, Leyani told the students, "I have a clue about what the next shape in the book is." The children looked at her expectantly and Leyani continued, "Listen to my clue and see if you can guess: The next shape has three sides and three corners." Leyani paused and then asked, "Can you guess what shape is on the next page?"

"A triangle!" Jorge predicted enthusiastically. Some of the other students looked at him quizzically.

"A circle?" Kaisha said tentatively.

"Let's find out," Leyani said and turned the page.

"Triangle," several students said in unison.

As with the previous spread, Leyani asked the children to report what they noticed. After talking with them about the pyramids, trees, mountains, cat's ears, eyes on the jack-o'-lantern, witch's hat, and bird's beak, she read the text and had them find the items described.

Leyani continued in this way for the rest of the book, giving them a hint first for a few of the shapes, choosing those she thought they could guess. For example, after discussing the circle page, Leyani asked the students to predict the next shape. She gave them a clue: "It's a squished circle." Leyani held her hands up to enclose a circular shape and then demonstrated squishing her hands together.

"Oval!" several students called out.

As she read, the children eagerly made many observations about the examples shown on each spread and also about the illustrations.

After finishing the book, Leyani said, "The title of the book we just read is *When a Line Bends . . . a Shape Begins,* so I thought about an activity that would help you think more about shapes that you can make from a line." Leyani held up a pipe cleaner and said, "What could I do with my line?"

"You could bend it," Acacia said.

"You could make it curly," Eduardo said.

"Do you think I could make it into a circle?" Leyani asked. Several students nodded. Some looked like they weren't sure. Leyani held the pipe cleaner at both ends and started to curve it.

"Keep going," Mallika said. Leyani completed the circle, holding together the two ends of the pipe cleaner. The students clapped.

"What other shapes could I make?" Leyani asked. No one had a suggestion, so Leyani showed them how she could shape the pipe cleaner into a rectangle. She straightened the pipe cleaner and then, as the children watched, she shaped it into an oval, then a triangle, then a square, and finally a heart.

"Can we do it?" Kaisha asked.

"Absolutely," Leyani answered. "I'll give you each your own pipe cleaner so you can explore making different shapes." Leyani distributed a pipe cleaner to each student. The children worked in different ways. Some bent their pipe cleaners into curly or zigzag segments. Others tried making a circle and Leyani helped those who were having difficulty. When Raul became frustrated with trying to make a triangle, Leyani helped him complete the task. Fawziya and Acacia figured out by themselves how to make a heart, and they helped others who needed it. Leyani noticed that Jesus worked methodically, carefully straightening his pipe cleaner after making each shape before starting a new one. Children made creations other than the shapes introduced in the book: Christian made a mustache; Melody made a crown; Queenie formed one end of the pipe cleaner into a small circle and explained that it was for blowing bubbles. As the children explored, they talked with one another about what they were making.

When it was time to stop, Leyani asked the students to report the shapes they made.

"I made a circle," Hallie said proudly.

"I made a triangle and a heart," Bayard said.

"I made a heart, too!" Purna said.

Before ending the lesson, Leyani collected the pipe cleaners, assuring the children that they would be able to take them home at the end of the day. She told them, "The ends are sharp and I want to be sure that you won't poke yourselves or anyone else."

Leyani did the same lesson with first graders and found it went just as well. After teaching the lessons, Leyani commented that there was so much to discuss in the children's book that she could read it multiple times to the children and they would still be involved. Leyani said, "It took a while for the kindergartners to sit and discuss every item on every page. It might make more sense for them to spread the reading over several days, reading only one or two pages at a time."

# Who Sank the Boat?

*Taught by Marilyn Burns*

Pamela Allen's book *Who Sank the Boat?* (1996) is about a cow, a donkey, a sheep, a pig, and a tiny mouse who decide to go for a row in the bay. The animals get into the boat one at a time, and each time the boat almost capsizes. Finally, the mouse causes the boat to sink. The story and delightful illustrations capture children's imaginations. Marilyn Burns reads this book to a kindergarten class in this lesson. She uses Cuisenaire rods to represent the animals to help the children visualize combinations of five.

## MATERIALS

Cuisenaire rods, regular or jumbo, 1 of each
color

Marilyn gathered the kindergarten children into a circle on the rug and showed them the cover of *Who Sank the Boat?* Several commented about boats they had been in. Some wanted to talk about toy boats they had. Marilyn told them that she was interested in their experiences with boats. "But right now," she said, "I'd like to read you the story about this boat."

Marilyn introduced the characters in the story, showing the class the picture of the cow, donkey, sheep, pig, and mouse walking on their hind legs toward the dock. Earlier in the class she had noticed Kyle, Alex, and Scott comparing the heights of two wooden figures and arguing about which figure would be taller if they weren't wearing hats. Marilyn told the class about the boys' discussion and then asked, "How do the sizes of the animals compare in this story?"

127

After some discussion, the general opinion seemed to be that cows are really bigger than donkeys, even though the donkey was a little taller in the picture, that sheep and pigs are about the same size, and that the mouse is the smallest.

In order to provide the students with a concrete reference while she read the story, Marilyn decided to draw from the class box of jumbo Cuisenaire rods. She removed an orange rod from the box and held it up for the class. "Since you think that the cow is the largest animal," she said, "I'm going to use an orange rod to represent it. What color rod should I use for the donkey?"

The children were familiar with the rods, and several suggested the blue rod. Marilyn removed a blue rod and held it next to the orange one, so the children could compare their lengths. "Why?" she asked.

"Because it's pretty big and close to the orange," Conner answered.

When Marilyn asked what color rod they should use for the sheep, Katy suggested yellow. "It's littler, but not real little," she said. The class was willing to accept her choice.

"What about for the pig?" Marilyn then asked.

"It looks the same," Mitch said. "Use another yellow." Marilyn followed Mitch's suggestion. Then she asked about the mouse.

About half the children answered, "A white rod."

Marilyn stood the rods in a row in front of her to represent the five animals and continued with the story: "They were good friends, and one warm sunny morning, for no particular reason, they decided to go for a row in the bay. Do you know who sank the boat?"

Some of the children called out guesses, and Marilyn reminded them about raising their hands. She called on several children to offer their predictions and then called on Kyle.

"I know who sank the boat," he said. "I know the story."

To find out whether anyone else knew the story, Marilyn responded, "So Kyle and I already know for sure who sank the boat. Does anyone else know?" No one responded.

"Let's not tell," Marilyn said to Kyle. "Let's see if they can figure it out from the story." Kyle nodded his agreement.

Alex raised his hand. "Can we lie down and listen to the story?" he asked.

"Yeah, like this," Scott said, lying down in the circle. Several of the children, all boys, proceeded to lie down. This class had twice as many boys as girls, and they were an active bunch. Marilyn asked the boys to sit up and return to their places on the circle.

Before returning to the book, Marilyn asked the class, "How many animals are in the boat now?"

Several children answered simultaneously: "None." "It's empty." "Zero."

Marilyn reminded the children again about raising their hands and then asked, "How many are waiting on the dock to get into the boat?" Most of the children raised their hands. Marilyn called on Judy, who answered correctly.

Marilyn continued reading the rhyme that describes the cow getting into the boat: "Was it the cow who almost fell in, when she tilted the boat and made such a din?" The cow almost makes the boat capsize, but the next page reveals that all is safe.

Marilyn moved the orange rod to one side to indicate it was now in the boat and asked, "How many animals are now in the boat? How many are still waiting on the dock?" Some children knew the answers immediately, others needed to count the rods, and some just weren't interested in the questions and waited for Marilyn to resume reading.

The story is cleverly presented so that a moment of panic accompanies each rhyme as an animal gets into the boat and almost sinks it. But when the page is turned, all is calm. Marilyn continued reading, moving the rods and talking with the children about how many animals were in the boat and how many were still on the dock.

At the end of the story, the tiny mouse leaps off the dock into the boat—and sinks it. The children were delighted.

"I have a question," Marilyn said. "How could a tiny mouse sink the boat after the four larger animals didn't?"

The class got quiet as children thought about the question. Hands started to go up, but Marilyn waited so all the children would have a chance to think about the question. Finally, she called on Alex.

"It's because he jumped into the boat, and he wasn't careful," he said.

"Yeah," J. P. added. "You're not supposed to jump when you get into a boat."

"That was my idea, too," Katy said.

"Does anyone have a different idea about why the mouse sank the boat?" Marilyn asked.

Maureen raised her hand. Always thoughtful, she replied, "It was just too much. It wasn't the mouse's fault. It was just too much for the boat."

Children's number sense develops over time from many experiences, and it's important to provide such experiences as often as possible. *Who Sank the Boat?* provides the chance for children to think about the combinations of five in the context of a story. Using the rods allows children to visualize the combinations.

# Blackline Master

*Ten Flashing Fireflies* Work Mat

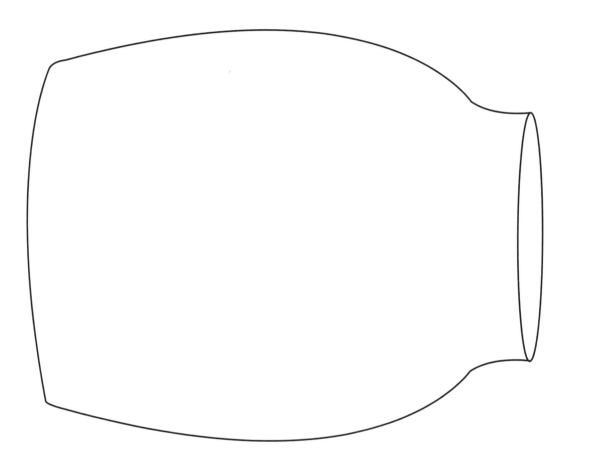

# References

Allen, Pamela. 1996. *Who Sank the Boat?* New York: Puffin.

Baker, Keith. 1999. *Quack and Count.* New York: Harcourt Brace.

Brisson, Pat. 1993. *Benny's Pennies.* Illus. Bob Barner. New York: Bantam Doubleday Dell Books for Young Readers.

Carle, Eric. 1972. *Rooster's Off to See the World.* New York: Scholastic.

Crews, Donald. 1995. *Ten Black Dots.* New York: Mulberry.

Dodds, Dayle Ann. 1994. *The Shape of Things.* Illus. Julie Lacome. Cambridge, MA: Candlewick.

Florian, Douglas. 2000. *A Pig Is Big.* New York: Greenwillow.

Geringer, Laura. 1985. *A Three Hat Day.* Illus. Arnold Lobel. New York: HarperCollins.

Greene, Rhonda Gowler. 1997. *When a Line Bends . . . a Shape Begins.* Illus. James Kaczman. Boston: Houghton Mifflin.

Hague, Kathleen. 1999. *Ten Little Bears: A Counting Rhyme.* Illus. Michael Hague. New York: Morrow Junior.

Harris, Trudy. 2000. *Pattern Fish.* Illus. Anne Canevari Green. Brookfield, CT: Millbrook.

Hong, Lily Toy. 1993. *Two of Everything.* Morton Grove, IL: Albert Whitman.

Lionni, Leo. 1995. *Inch by Inch.* New York: HarperTrophy.

Merriam, Eve. 1993. *12 Ways to Get to 11.* Illus. Bernie Karlin. New York: Aladdin.

Moore, Inga. 1991. *Six-Dinner Sid.* New York: Aladdin.

Ochiltree, Dianne. 1998. *Cats Add Up!* Illus. Marcy Dunn-Ramsey. New York: Scholastic.

O'Connell, Jennifer. 2002. *Ten Timid Ghosts on a Christmas Night.* New York: Scholastic.

Reid, Margarette S. 1990. *The Button Box.* Illus. Sarah Chamberlain. New York: Dutton Children's.

Shulevitz, Uri. 2003. *One Monday Morning.* New York: Farrar, Straus and Giroux.

Silverstein, Shel. 1974. *Where the Sidewalk Ends.* New York: HarperCollins.

Slater, Teddy. 1999. *Ready or Not, Here I Come!* Illus. Gioia Fiammenghi. New York: Scholastic.

Sturges, Philemon. 1995. *Ten Flashing Fireflies.* Illus. Anna Vojtech. New York: North-South.

Williams, Sue. 1998. *Let's Go Visiting.* Illus. Julie Vivas. New York: Harcourt Brace.

Wise, William. 1993. *Ten Sly Piranhas: A Counting Story in Reverse.* Illus. Victoria Chess. New York: Dial Books for Young Readers.

Wood, Audrey. 1984. *The Napping House.* Illus. Don Wood. New York: Harcourt Brace.

# Index

addition
  with cats, lesson, 15–20
  with combinations of animals,
    lessons, 28–34, 76–80
  with dots, lesson, 95–97
  11 (eleven), lesson on different
    combinations equal to, 112–18
  multiple answers, problem-
    solving lesson with, 35–44
  sum of 7 (seven), lesson on dif-
    ferent ways of showing, 60–67
Allen, Pamela, 127

Baker, Keith, 60
"Band-Aids," lesson, 112–18
*Benny's Pennies,* lesson, 1–9
  kindergarten class, sharing
    book with, 8–9
  first grade class, sharing book
    with, 1–8
  bigger than/smaller than, lesson,
    54–59
Blackline Master, 131–33
Brisson, Pat, 1
Burns, Marilyn, 127–29
*Button Box, The,* lesson, 10–14

Caldecott Honor Book award,
  21–22
Carle, Eric, 76
*Cats Add Up!,* lesson, 15–20
circles

forming, 123–26
  identifying, 82–86
comparing
  bigger than/smaller than, lesson,
    54–59
  buttons, lesson, 10–14
  multiple answers, problem-
    solving lesson with, 39–40
  sizes of animals, lesson,
    127–29
counting
  buttons, lesson, 10–14
  combinations of animals, lesson,
    28–34, 76–80
  11 (eleven), different ways of
    counting to, 112–18
  and graphing, lesson, 45–49
  money, lesson, 1–9
  to 100 (one hundred), lesson,
    68–75
  from 1 (one) to 10 (ten) and
    from 10 (ten) to 1 (one),
    lesson, 98–104
  reverse, lessons, 98–104,
    105–7
crescents, forming, 123–26
Crews, Donald, 92
Cuisenaire rods, 127–29

describing
  buttons, lesson, 10–14
  coins, lesson, 8–9

137

diamonds
  forming, 123–26
  identifying, 83
Dodds, Dayle Ann, 81
dots, representing objects with, 92–97
doubling, 2–3
doubling numbers, 119–22

equations. *See* number sentences
equivalence, 62
even, odd, 39

Florian, Douglas, 54

Genolio, Marge, 92–97
geometry
  shapes, lesson on bending lines to form, 123–26
  shapes, lesson on identifying, 81–86
Geringer, Laura, 108
gradually, defining, 35–36
graphing and counting, lesson, 45–49
Greene, Rhonda Gowler, 123

Hague, Kathleen, 98
Harris, Trudy, 50
hearts, forming, 123–26
Hong, Lily Toy, 119
Hong, Min, 112, 114–18
house, origami, 37–38

illustrations, of number sentences, 64–67
*Inch by Inch*, lesson, 21–27
inches, introductory lesson for, 21–27

larger than/smaller than, lesson, 54–59
length. *See* linear measurement
*Let's Go Visiting*, 28–34
linear measurement, inches, introductory lesson for, 21–27

lines, lesson on forming shapes from, 123–26
Lionni, Leo, 21
Lobel, Arnold, 108

measurement. *See also individual categories or units*
  inches, introductory lesson for, 21–27
Merriam, Eve, 112
money
  coins, lesson on identifying, 8–9
  counting and handling, lesson, 1–9
Moore, Inga, 87
multiple answers, problems solving lesson with, 35–44

*Napping House, The,* lesson, 35–44
numbers, doubling, 119–22
number sentences
  addition and subtraction with cats, lesson, 15–20
  with combinations of animals, lessons, 30–34, 76–80
  11 (eleven), different combinations equal to, 112–18
  illustrating, lesson, 64–67
  multiple answers, problem-solving lesson with, 35–44
  10 (ten), lesson on combinations of, 100–104
  using dots to represent numbers on a page, 92–97

Ochiltree, Dianne, 15
O'Connell, Jennifer, 98
octagons, forming, 123–26
100 (one hundred), lesson on skip counting to, 68–75
*One Monday Morning,* lesson, 45–49
origami house, 37–38
ovals, forming, 123–26

parallelograms, identifying, 83
*Pattern Fish,* lesson, 50–53

patterns
  doubling numbers, 119–22
  repeating, lessons, 50–53,
    76–80, 87–91
  with shapes, 82–84
  6s (sixes), repeating, 87–91
*Pig Is Big, A,* lesson, 54–59
predicting with repeating patterns, lesson, 50–53, 78–79
probability, 109–11

*Quack and Count,* lesson,
  60–67

*Ready or Not, Here I Come!,*
  lesson, 68–75
rectangles
  forming, 123–26
  identifying, 83–86
Reid, Margarette S., 10
restating problems, 88
reverse counting, lessons,
  98–104, 105–7
*Rooster's Off to See the World,*
  lesson, 76–80
Rotz, Leyani von
  *Cats Add Up!,* lesson by, 15–20
  *Inch by Inch,* lesson by, 21–27
  *Let's Go Visiting,* lesson by,
    28–34
  *Pattern Fish,* lesson by, 50–53
  *Pig Is Big, A,* lesson by, 54–59
  *Quack and Count,* lesson by,
    60–67
  *Ready or Not, Here I Come!,*
    lesson by, 68–75
  *Shape of Things, The,* lesson
    by, 81–86
  *Ten Flashing Fireflies,* lesson
    by, 98–104
  *When a Line Bends...a Shape
    Begins,* lesson by, 123–26

*Shape of Things, The,* lesson,
  81–86
shapes
  bending lines to form, lesson,
    123–26

  identifying, lesson on, 81–86
Sheffield, Stephanie
  *Benny's Pennies* lesson by, 1–9
  *Napping House, The,* lesson by,
    35–44
  *One Monday Morning,* lesson
    by, 45–49
  *Six-Dinner Sid,* lesson by,
    87–91
  *Ten Sly Piranhas,* lesson by,
    105–7
  *12 Ways to Get to 11* and
    "Band-Aids," lesson by,
    112–14
  *Two of Everything,* lesson by,
    119–22
Shulevitz, Uri, 45
Silverstein, Shel, 112
*Six-Dinner Sid,* lesson, 87–91
skip counting
  to 100 (one hundred), lesson,
    68–75
  repeating patterns, lessons,
    50–53, 76–80, 87–91
  by 6s (sixes), lesson, 87–91
Slater, Teddy, 68
smaller than/bigger than, lesson,
  54–59
snap cubes, 45–49
sorting
  buttons, lesson, 10–14
  coins, 5–8
squares
  forming, 123–26
  identifying, 82–86
stars, forming, 123–26
Sturges, Philemon, 98
subtraction
  with cats, lesson, 15–20
  number sentences with, lesson,
    105–7
symbols, problem-solving with,
  109–11

Tank, Bonnie, 10–14, 108–11
t-charts, 101–4, 120–21
*Ten Black Dots,* lesson,
  92–97

*Ten Flashing Fireflies,* lesson,
  98–104
  with kindergarten class,
    98–100
  with first grade class, 100–104
  work mat, Blackline Master
    for, 131–33
10 (ten) lesson on combinations
  of, 98–104
*Ten Little Bears,* 98
*Ten Sly Piranhas,* 105–7
*Ten Timid Ghosts on a
  Christmas Night,* 98
*Three Hat Day, A,* lesson,
  108–11
Torres, Olga, 76–80, 92
triangles
  forming, 123–26
  identifying, 83–86

*12 Ways to Get to11,* lesson,
  112–18
twice as much, explaining
  phrase, 2
*Two of Everything,* lesson,
  119–22

verbalize thinking, developing
  students' ability to, 89–90

*When a Line Bends . . . a Shape
  Begins,* lesson, 123–26
*Where the Sidewalk Ends,*
  112
*Who Sank the Boat?,* lesson,
  127–29
Williams, Sue, 28
Wise, William, 105–7
Wood, Audrey, 35